KIDS STUFF
RUSSIAN

KIDS STUFF
RUSSIAN

Easy Russian Phrases for You and Your Kids

Therese Slevin Pirz

BILINGUAL KIDS SERIES

CHOU CHOU PRESS
58 Seaford Place
Bluffton, SC 29909

Cataloging data: Pirz, Therese Slevin
                          Kids stuff Russian: Easy Russian phrases for you and
                     your kids.
                     Chou Chou Press, 2001
                          204 p. illus

                          Description: A collection of children's basic phrases
                     arranged by activity and rendered in Russian and English.
                     Pronunciation is given for the Russian sentences.

                          1. Russian language 2. Russian phrases 3. Russian
                     conversation and phrase book 4. Homeschooling I. Title.
                     II. Title: Easy Russian phrases for you and your kids.
                     III. Series: Bilingual Kids

                                                                          491

Printed in the United States of America, 2003

First Edition.
Library of Congress Catalog No. 2001130806

ISBN   0-9606140-6-0

Order direct from the publisher:

                          Chou Chou Press

                     58 Seaford Place
                     Bluffton, SC 29909

May the Lord shed His
Light on us.

CONTENTS
ACKNOWLEDGMENTS
PREFACE

VOCABULARY

Note: Where transcription is not given in the text, the accented syllable is indicated by **bold face** type or underlining.

Child's name:_____

Received this book from:_____

Occasion:_____ ' Date:_____

First indication of child's understanding Russian:_____

_____

Child's first Russian word:_____

Child's favorite Russian word:_____

Favorite Russian books or stories:_____

_____

_____

Favorite Russian songs:_____

_____

Favorite Russian movies or videos:_____

_____

_____

Favorite things to do in Russian:_____

_____

_____

_____

Favorite Russian foods:_____

_____

ACKNOWLEDGMENTS

Ardith El-Kareh is the first of several persons that I would like to thank for contributing to the start and completion of this book. Ardith inspired me to get going and keep at the daily writing of the manuscript.

I wish to thank Marietta Bagrash, professor of Russian at Lehigh University, and Donna Faturos who proof read the beginnings of the manuscript.

Irena Rook, a linguistics major at the University of Moscow, is an outstanding, professional translator and proofreader who undertook this project with a diligence and thoroughness that fill me with admiration and gratitude.

I have never met any of these fine people in person! I don't even know what they look like. All contact and communication have been done by computer or telephone. Would that we could all meet, and enjoy the results of our efforts together.

I thank them all for their contributions to the text. I hope they are pleased with the results.

Finally, my thanks, as always, to my husband, Joe, for his patience, encouragement and support throughout this project.

PREFACE

This book covers the range of children's interests from infancy to teens. It is meant to cover not so much the calendar age of children, but rather their activities and interests regardless of what birthdays they have passed. This perspective is taken because children develop at different rates. It is hard to predict where they will be in their development and what their experiences will be at any particular age.

The author has researched many books in preparation for writing the *KIDS STUFF SERIES*, and has found this series to be unique among the vast array of books intended for children learning foreign languages. Like other books in the *KIDS STUFF SERIES*, <u>Kids Stuff Russian</u> translates ideas, phrases and sentences that parents and children wish to express in Russian. The user is able to speak, carry on a conversation, and model sentences that can be used in replying to others.

At whatever age parents and children begin their foreign language adventure, this book will be an invaluable guide on the journey.

Enjoy this book and your children. Good luck and have fun. Желаю успеха!

Nice to be a guest, but there's no place like home.

В ГОСТЯХ ХОРОШО, А ДОМА ЛУЧШЕ

Приветствие   Greetings

Start your day and your conversations here. Saying the first few words in Russian will help you build momentum to continue speaking Russian for the rest of the day. Hearing and speaking Russian will make you feel cheerful especially when it is spoken by you or to you by your little one.

Здравствуйте.
ZdrAHstvooytyih.

Hello!

Алло!
AhlAW!

Hello!
(Answering the telephone)

Слушаю. Кто у телефона?
SlOOshahyoo. Ktaw oo tihlihfAWnah?

Hello! Who's speaking?
(Answering the telephone.)

Это я! Это........ говорит.
EHtah yah! EHtah........... gahvahrEEt.

Speaking! (It is I.)
This is.........speaking.

13

Я тебе перезвоню.
Yah tihbYEH pihrihzvahnYOO.

I'll call you back.

Позвони....
PahzvahnEE...

Call...

До свидания.
Dah sveedAHnyih.

Goodbye.

Всего хорошего!
FsyihvAW khahrAWshihvah!

All the best!

Доброе утро.
DAWbrahyih OOtrah.

Good morning.

Добрый день.
DAWbruiy dyehn'.

Good day. Hi!

Добрый вечер.
DAWbruiy vYEHchihr.

Good evening.
(Greeting)

Спокойной ночи.
SpahkAWnoy nAWchee.

Good night.

До завтра!
Dah zAHftrah!

Until tomorrow!

Войди! (после стука в дверь)
VahydEE!

Come in!
(after knocking)

Рад/ Рада/ тебя видеть. (m/f)
Raht/ RAHdah/ tihbYAH vEEdiht'.

I'm glad to see you.

Я рад /-а тебе. (m/f)
Yah raht/ rAHdah tihbYEH.

It's good to see you.
(long absence)

Как дела?
Kahk dyihlAH?

How goes it! How are
things?

Как поживаешь?
Kahk pahzheevAHihsh?

How are you?

Как ты себя чувствуешь?
Kahk tui sihbYAH chOOstvooihsh?

How do you feel?

Выздоравливай.
VuizdahrAHvleevahy.

Get well soon.

У меня всё.
Oo mnYAH fsyaw.

I'm all right.

(Очень) хорошо спасибо.
(AWchihn') khahrahshAW spahsEEbah.

(Very) well, thanks.

Что нового?
Shtaw nAWvahvah?

What's new?

(У меня) ничего нового!
(Oo mnYAH) neechihvAW nAWvahvah!

Nothing new
(with me)!

Я буду скучать без тебя.
Yah bOOdoo skoochAHt' byehs tihbYAH.

I will miss you.

Скучал/-а ли ты без меня? (m/f)
SkoochAHl/-ah lee tui byehs mnYAH?

Did you miss me?

Что ты мне привёз (m)/ привезла (f)/?
Shtaw tui mnYEH preevYAWs/
preevyihzlAH/?

What did you bring me?

Обними меня.
AhbneemEE mnYAH.

Give me a hug.

Поцелуй меня!
PahtsihlOOy mnYAH!

Give me a kiss!

Что я могу сделать для тебя?
Shtaw yah mahgOO zdYEHlaht' dlyah
tihbYAH?

What can I do for you?

15

GREETINGS_____

Помочь тебе?   Do you need any help?
PahmAWch' tihbYEH?

Мне плохо. Не хорошо.   Not so good. Not so well.
MnYEH plAWkhah. Nih khahrahshAW.

Так себе.   So so.
Tahk sihbYEH.

До скорого. Пока.   See you later. So long.
Dah skAWrahvah. PahkAH.

До скорого! До свидания.   See you soon! Goodbye.
Dah skAWrahvah! Dah sveedAHnyih.

Желаю хорошо провести время!   Have a good time!
ZhihlAHyoo khahrahshAW prahvyihs-
tEE vrYEHmyih!

Счастливого пути!   Have a good trip!
ShahstlEEvahvah pootEE!

Передай привет ....   (+ Dat.).   Say hello to...
PihrihdAHy preevYEHt...

Помаши рукой.   Wave good-bye.
PahmahshEE rookOY.

Извини.   Excuse me.
EezveenEE.

Прости!   I beg your pardon!
PrahstEE!

Всего доброго! (or) Желаю успеха!   Good luck!
FsyihvAW dAWbrahvah! (or)
ZhihlAHyoo oospYEHkhah!

Слава Богу!   Thank God!
SlAHvah bAWgoo!

Благослови тебя Бог!
BlahgahslahvEE tihbYAH bawk!

God bless you!

Поздравляю!
PahzdrahvlYAHyoo!

Congratulations!

С днем рождения!
Zdnyawm rahzhdYEHneeyih!

Happy Birthday!

С рождеством Христовым!
SrahzhdyihstvAWm KhreestAWvuim!

Merry Christmas!

С Новым Годом!
SnAWvuim gAWdahm!

Happy New Year!

Будь здоров/-а! (m/f)
Boot' zdahrAWf/ zdahrAWvah!

Bless you!

Твоё здоровье!
TvahYAW zdahrAWv'yih!

To your health!

Пожалуйста.
PahzhAHloostah.

Please.

(Нет) Спасибо. Большое спасибо.
(Nyeht) SpahsEEbah. Bahl'shAWyih
spahsEEbah.

(No), thank you.
Thanks a lot.

Спасибо за всё, что ты для меня
сделал /-а. (m/f)
SpahsEEbah zah fsyaw, shtaw tui dlyah
mnYAH zdYEHlahl/-ah.

Thank you for all you
have done.

Пожалуйста. (or) Не за что.
PahzhAHloostah. (or) NYEH zah shtaw.

You're welcome.

Добро пожаловать!
DahbrAW pahzhAHlahvaht'!

Welcome!

Очень/ рад/ рада/ с тобой
познакомиться.   (m/f)
AWchihn'/ raht/ rAHdah/ stahbOY
pahznahkAWmeet'sah.

I'm glad to meet you.

Ты говоришь по-русски?
Tui gahvahrEEsh pah-rOOskee?

Do you speak Russian?

Как сказать...?
Kahk skahzAHt'...?

How do you say....?

Я (не) говорю по-русски.
Yah (nih) gahvahrYOO pah-rOOskee.

I (don't) speak Russian.

Как тебя зовут?
Kahk tihbYAH zahvOOt?

What is your name?

Меня зовут...
MnYAH zahvOOt...

My name is ...

Где ты живёшь?
Gdyeh tui zheevYAWsh?

Where do you live?

Счастливого пути.
ShahstlEEvahvah pootEE.

Have a good trip.

Добрый день!
DAWbruiy dyehn'!

Have a nice day!

18

we must, we must wash up, From morning until night.

Нада, нада умываться, По утрам и вечерам.*

Ванная комната   The Bathroom

Every family member knows how much time is spent in the bathroom showering, bathing, singing, soaking, admiring.... A good time to practice your Russian looking in the mirror or aloud in the shower.

Сходи в туалет. S'khahdEE ftooahlYEHt.	Go to the bathroom. (toilet)
Помой/ руки/ уши/. Умойся. PahmOY/ rOOkee/OOshee. OomOYsah.	Wash your /hands/ ears/. Wash your face.
Скажи мне,/ Ты мне сказал/-а, (m/f) когда тебе нужно... SkahzhEE mnYEH, /Tui mnYEH skah- zAHl/-ah,/ kahgdAH tihbYEH nOOzhnah...	Tell me/ You told me/ when you have...
...сходить в туалет. ...s'khahdEEt' ftooahlYEHt.	...to go to the toilet.

19

Спусти за собой (воду).
SpoostEE zah sahbOY (vAWdoo).

Flush the toilet.

Закрой туалетную крышку.
ZahkrOY tooahlYEHtnooyoo
krUIshkoo.

Put down the seat.

Давай помоем руки.
DahvAHy pahmAWihm rOOkee.

Let's wash up.

У тебя грязное лицо. Вымой его.
Oo tihbYAH grYAHznahyih leetsAW.
VUImoy yihvAW.

Your face is dirty.
Wash it.

Не забудь помыть руки
(перед едой/ ужином).
Nih zahbOOt' pahmUIt' rOOkee
(pYEHrihd yihdOY/ OOzheenahm).

Don't forget to wash your
hands (before a meal/ or
dinner).

Ты помыл/-а шею? (m/f)
Tui pahmUIl/-ah shYEHyoo?

Did you wash your neck?

Почисти зубы после еды.
PahchEEstee zOObui pAWslih yihdUI.

Brush your teeth after
eating.

Прочисти ниткой между зубами.
PrahchEEstee nEEtkoy mYEHzhdoo
zoobAHmee.

Floss between your teeth.

Твоя зубная щётка на раковине.
TvahYAH zoobNAHyah schYAWtkah
nah rAHkahveenyih.

Your toothbrush is on the
sink.

Помни, что надо почистить зубы.
PAWmnee, shtaw nAHdah pah-
chEEsteet' zOObui.

Remember to brush your
teeth.

Ты не вымыл/-а лицо. (m/f)
Tui nih vUImuil/-ah leetsAW.

You didn't wash your face.

Ты/ весь/ вся/ чистый/-ая? (m/f)
Tui/ vyehs'/ fsyah/ chEEstuiy/-ahyah/?

Are you all clean?

Ты выгладишь чистым.
Tui vUIglahdeesh chEEstuim.

You look clean.

У тебя чистые лицо и руки.
Oo tihbYAH chEEstuiyih leetsAW
ee rOOkee.

Your face and hands are clean.

Тебе нужно принять ванну.
TihbYEH nOOzhnah preenYAHt'
vAHnnoo.

You need to take a bath.

/Открой/ Закрой/ кран.
/AhtkrOY/ ZahkrOY/ krahn.

Turn the faucet/ on/ off/.

Ты принимаешь ванну ?
Tui preeneemAHihsh vAHnnoo?

Are you taking a bath?

Я готовлю для тебя ванну.
Yah gahtAWvlyoo dlyah tihbYAH
vAHnnoo.

I'm running a bath for you.

Видишь, как течёт вода ?
VEEdeesh, kahk tihchYAWt vahdAH ?

See the water run?

Вода слишком/ горячая/ холодная/.
VahdAH slEEshkahm/ gahrYAHch-
ahyah/ khahlAWdnahyah/.

The water is too/ hot/ cold/.

Не наливай в ванну слишком много воды.
Nih nahleevAHy vvAHnnoo slEEshkahm mnAWgah vahdUI.

Don't fill the tub with too much water.

Я мою твою спину, колени и животик.
Yah mAWyoo tvahYOO spEEnoo,
kahlYEHnee ee zheevAWteek.

I'm washing your back, knees and tummy.

Как ты брызгаешь!
Kahk tui bruizgAHihsh!

How you splash!

Помойся с мылом.
PahmOYsah s'mUIlahm.

Use soap.

Мыло хорошо пахнет, но оно скользкое.
MUIlah khahrahshAW pAHkhnyiht,
naw ahnAW skAWl'skahyih.

The soap smells good,
but it is slippery.

Не так много:
Nih tahk mnAWgah:
   мыла, (mUIlah), воды, (vahdUI)
   зубной пасты, (zoobnOY pAHstui)
   дезодоранта. (dihzahdahrAHntah).

Not so much:

   soap, water,
   toothpaste,
   deodorant.

Как следует вытрись, прежде чем
выйти из ванной.
Kahk slYEHdooiht vUItrees, prYEHzhdyih chyehm vUIytee eez vAHnnoy.

Dry yourself well before
leaving the bath room.

Спусти воду.
SpoostEE vAWdoo.

Empty the tub.

Вычисти (or Вымой) ванну.
VUIcheestee (or VUImoy) vAHnnoo.

Clean the tub.

Сложи полотенце.
SlahzhEE pahlahtYEHntsih.

Fold the towel.

Положи полотенце в стирку.
PahlahzhEE pahlahtYEHntsih
fstEErkoo.

Put the towel in the
laundry.

Повесь полотенце.
PahvYEHs' pahlahtYEHntsih.

Hang up the towel.

Ты выключил/-а свет? (m/f)
Tui vUIklyoocheel/-ah svyeht?

Did you turn out the
light?

Ты хотел/-а бы принять ванну? (m/f)
Tui khahtYEHl/-ah bui preenYAHt'
vAHnnoo?

Would you like to take
a bath?

Нет. Я не хочу (принимать ванну).
Nyeht. Yah nih khahchOO (preenee-MAHT' vAHnnoo).

No. I don't want to
(take a bath).

Тебе нужно/ постричься/ побриться/.
TihbYEH nOOzhnah/ pahstrEEch'-sah/ pahbrEEt'sah/.

You need/ a haircut/ to
shave/.

Потом помой голову!
PahtAWm pahmOY gAWlahvoo!

Wash your hair later!

Ты хорошо выглядишь.
Tui khahrahshAW vUIglyihdeesh.

You look good.

* from page 19 "Мойдодыр" by Tchukovsky

Leave well enough alone.

От добра добра не ищут

Одевание   Getting Dressed

Is it to be the cowboy outfit or the space suit this morning? When you are in a hurry these are not options. Perhaps, instead, when your little girl dresses her dolls, or your little guy is playing with his action figures, you and they can try some of these phrases.

Вставай! Уже пора вставать!
FstahvAHy! OozhYEH pahrAH
fstahvAHt'!

Get up! It's time to get up!

Я меняю твой подгузник.
Yah mihnYAHyoo tvoy pahdgOOzneek.

I'm changing your diaper.

Просунь руку в рукав.
PrahsOOn' rOOkoo vrookAHf.

Put your hand through
the sleeve.

Я надеваю правую туфлю.
Yah nahdihvAHyoo prAHvooyoo
TOOflyoo.

I'm putting on your right
shoe.

На тебе не тот ботинок.
Nah tihbYEH nih tawt bahtEEnahk.

You have the wrong shoe on.

Застегни рубашку.
ZahstihgnEE roobAHshkoo.

Button your shirt.

Я не могу решить, что надеть.
Yah nih mahgOO rihshEEt', shtaw nahdYEHt'.

I can't decide what to wear.

Ты хочешь надеть белую или синюю блузку?
Tui khAWchish nahdYEHt' bYEHl-ooyoo EElee sEEnyooyoo blOOskoo?

Do you want to put on the white or the blue blouse?

Где твоя шляпа?
Gdyeh tvahYAH shlYAHpah?

Where is your hat?

Застегни молнию на куртке.
ZahstihgnEE mAHlneeyoo nah kOOrtkyih.

Close the zipper on your jacket.

Ищи свои перчатки.
EeschEE svahEE pihrchAHtkee.

Look for your gloves.

Папа пошёл на работу.
PAHpah pahshAWl nah rahbAWtoo.

Daddy has gone to work.

Пора одеваться.
PahrAH ahdihvAHt'sah.

It's time to get dressed.

Нам нужно одеваться.
Nahm nOOzhnah ahdihvAHt'sah.

We have to get dressed.

Перестань кусать ногти!
PirihstAHn' koosAHt' nAWktee!

Stop biting your nails!

Надень нижнее бельё и брюки.
NahdYEHn' nEEzhnihyih bihl'YAW ee brYOOkee.

Put on your underpants and pants.

Надень новое пальто.
NahdYEHn' nAWvahyih pahl'tAW.

Wear your new coat.

Причешись.
PreechYEHshees.

Comb or Brush your hair.

Давай я тебя подстригу.
DahvAHy yah tihbYAH pahtstreegOO.

Let me trim your hair.

Щётка и расчёска на туалетном столе.
SchYAWtkah ee rahschYAWskah nah
tooahlYEHtnahm stahlYEH.

The brush and comb
are on the dresser.

(Хоть) переоденься.
(Khawt') pihrihahdYEHn'sah.

(At least) change your
clothes.

Можешь надеть футболку.
MAWzhihsh nahdYEHt' footbAWLkoo.

The T-shirt will be fine.

Как ты хорошо выглядишь!
Kahk tui khahrahshAW vUIglyihdeesh!

How nice you look!

Everyone to his own taste.

Как начей вкус

Время еды   Meal Time

"Beverages," "Desserts," and "Meats," pages in this book will help expand your food vocabulary. You can even pretend you and your children are a bird from the "Birds" page. Select the "Insects" birds find appetizing. (Something to do AFTER eating!)

Давайте кушать! Перестань играть.   Let's eat! Stop playing.
DahvAHytyih kOOshaht'!
PihrihstAHn' eegrAHt'.

Сейчас же ешь!   Eat now!
SihchAHs zhyeh yehsh!

Тебе хочется позавтракать?   Do you feel like eating
TihbYEH khAWchihtsah pahzAHvtrahkaht'?   breakfast?

Сейчас я не хочу.   I don't want to now.
SihchAHs yah nih khahchOO.

Иди за стол, пожалуйста   Come to the table, please.
EedEE zah stawl, pahzhAHloostah.

27

Когда мы будем обедать? KahgdAH mui bOOdihm ahbYEHdaht?	When are we having lunch?
Ты/ голоден/ голодна/? (m/f) Tui/ gAWLahdihn/ gahlahdnAH/?	Are you hungry?
Я (так)/ голоден/ голодна/. (m/f) Yah (tahk) /gAWLahdihn/ gahlahdnAH/.	I'm (so) hungry.
Я умираю с голоду! Yah oomeerAHyoo sgahlahdOO!	I'm starving!
Мне хочется пить. MnYEH khAWchihtsah peet'.	I'm thirsty.
Что бы ты хотел /-а поесть? (m/f) Shtaw bui tui khahtYEHl/-ah pahYEHst'?	What would you like to eat?
Ты хотел/ хотела/ бы что-нибудь поесть? Tui /khahtYEHl/ khahtYEHlah/ bui shtAW-neeboot'pahyehst'? (m/f)	Would you like something to eat?
Я возьму... Yah vahz'mOO...	I'll have...
Как на счёт ужина? Kahk nahs chYAWt OOzheenah?	What about dinner?
Что у нас на ужин? Shtaw oo nahs nah OOzheen?	What do we have for dinner?
Что ты делал/-а сегодня? (m/f) Shtaw tui dYEHahl/ dYEHahlah sihvAWdnyih?	What did you do today?
Ты ничего не ел/-а. (m/f) Tui neechihvAW nih YEHl/-ah.	You have not eaten anything.
Когда мы будем кушать? KahgdAH mui bOOdihm kOOshaht'?	When are we eating?

Кто хочет кушать?
Ktaw khAWchiht kOOshaht'?

Who wants to eat?

Ужин готов.
OOzheen gahtAWf.

Dinner is ready.

Давайте сядем (за стол).
DahvAHytyih sYAHdihm (zah stawl).

Let's sit down.

Сядь рядом/ со мной/ с ним/ с ней/.
Syaht' rYAHdahm/ sah mnoy/ sneem/
snyehy/.

Sit near/ me/ him/ her/.

Сядь (правильно).
Syaht' (prAHveel'nah).

Sit down (correctly).

Убери локти со стола.
OobihrEE lAWktee sah stahlAH.

Take your elbows off the table.

Давай перекусим.
DahvAHy pihrihkOOseem.

Let's have a snack.

Разогрей пиццу в микроволновке.
RahzahgrYEHy pEEtszoo fmeekrah-
vahlnAWvkyih.

Warm the pizza in the micro.

Ты хочешь бекон или картофель?
Tui khAWchihsh bYEHkahn EElee
kahrtAWfihl?

Do you want bacon or potatoes?

Возьми, пожалуйста.
Vahz'mEE, pahzhAHloostah.

Help yourself.

Возьми ещё немного.
Vahz'mEE yihschYAW nihmnAWgah.

Take some more.

Сделай себе сандвич.
ZdYEHlahy sihbYEH sAHndveech.

Make yourself a sandwich.

Можно мне ещё морковки?
MAWzhnah mnYEH yihschYAW
mahrkAWfkee?

May I have more carrots?

Хочешь добавки ?
KhAWchyish dahbAHvkee?

Do you want another
helping?

А мне что-нибудь осталось?
Ah mnYEH shtAW-neeboot'
ahstahlAWs'?

Is there any more left for
me?

Поделись печеньем.
PahdyehlEEs' pihchYEHn'yihm.

Share your cookie.

Я бы съел ещё немного каши.
Yah bui syehl yihschYAW nihmnAW-
gah kAHshee.

I'll take a little more cereal.

Хочу ещё порцию каши.
KhahchOO yihschYAW pAWrtseeyoo
kAHshee.

I want another helping of
cereal.

Мне достаточно.
MnYEH dahstAHtahchnah.

I am still hungry.

Я больше не хочу. Я сыт.
Yah bAWl'shih nih khahchOO. Yah siht.

I don't want any more.
 I'm full.

Можно попробовать немного?
MAWzhnah pahprAWbahvaht'
nihmnAWgah?

May I have a taste?

Да, чуть-чуть.
Dah, choot'-choot'.

Yes, a little.

Я тоже хочу.
Yah tAWzhyih khahchOO.

I want some too.

Что ты пьёшь?
Shtaw tui p'yawsh?

What are you drinking?

Что ты/ пил/ пила/? (m/f)
Shtaw tui/ peel/ peelAH/?

What did you drink?

Я больше не могу есть.
Yah bAWl'shih nih mahGOO yehst'.

I cannot eat any more.

Есть больше нечего.
Yehst'bAWl'shih nEEchihvoh.

There is no more.

Передай, пожалуйста, соль?
PihrihdAHy, pahzhAHloostah, sawl'?

Would you pass the salt?

Пользуйся вилкой, ножом, ложкой.
PAWl'zoosah vEElkoy, nahzhAWm,
lAWshkoy.

Use your fork, knife, spoon.

Не жми банан в руке.
Nih zhmEE bahnAHn vrOOkyih.

Don't squeeze the banana
in your hand.

Осторожно, не проглоти косточку.
AhstahrAWzhnah, nih prahglahtEE
kahstAWchkoo.

Be careful not to swallow
the pit.

Давай я порежу тебе мясо.
DahvAHy yah pahrihzhOO tihbYEH
mYAHsah.

Let me cut your meat.

Не пей так быстро молоко!
Nih pyey tahk bUIstrah mahlahkAW!

Don't drink your milk so
fast!

Накрывай бутылку.
NahkruivAHy bootUIlkoo.

Put the cover on the bottle.

Съешь немного. Пробуй это.
Syehsh nihmnAWgah. PrAWbooy EHtah.

Eat (just) a little. Try it.

Еда хорошо пахнет.
IhdAH khahrahshAW pAHkhnyiht.

The food smells good.

Это вкусно? Мне нравится.
EHtah fkOOsnah? MnYEH nrAHveetsah.

Is it tasty ? I like it.

Пудинг слишком/ сладкий/ солёный/.
POOdeenk slEEshkahm/ slAHtkeey/
sahlYAWnuiy/.

The pudding is too/ sweet/
salty/.

Соус очень/ горький/ кислый/ острый/.
Saws AWchihn'/ gAWr'keey/ kEEsluiy/
AWstruiy/.

The sauce is/ bitter/ sour/
spicy/.

Тебе нравится сыр?
TihbYEH nrAHveetsah suir?

Do you like the cheese?

Можно мне глоточек?
MAWzhnah mnYEH glahtAWchihk?

Can I have a sip?

Ешь шпинат.
Yehsh shpeenAHt.

Eat your spinach.

Мне нравятся бобы.
MnYEH nrAHvyiht'sah bahbUI.

I like green beans.

Ты можешь есть/ сам/ сама/. (m/f)
Tui mAWzhihsh yehst'/ sahm/ sAHmah/.

You can feed yourself.

Не говори сполным ртом.
Nih gahvahrEE spAHlnuim rtAWm.

Don't speak with your
mouth full.

Налей молоко в стакан.
NahlYEHy mahlahkAW fstahkAHn.

Pour the milk in the glass.

Режь хлеб осторожно.
Ryehzh' khlyehp ahstahrAWzhnah.

Cut the bread carefully.

Не наливай в стакан воды.
Nih nahleevAHy fstahkAHn vahdUI.

Don't fill the glass
with water.

Стакан полон.
StahkAHn pAWlahn.

The glass is full.

Ты пролил/-а молоко. (m/f)
Tui prahlEEl/ prahlihlAH mahlahkAW.

You spilt some milk.

Почему ты так много ешь?
PahchihmOO tui tahk mnAWgah yehsh?

Why do you eat so much?

Доешь ужин.
DahYEHsh OOzheen.

Finish your dinner.

Допей/ молоко/ апельсиновый сок/.
DahpYEHy/ mahlahkAW/ ahpihl'sEE-
nahvuiy sawk/.

Finish your /milk/ orange
juice/.

ты доел/-а? (m/f)
Tui dahYEHl/-ah?

Have you finished eating?

Ты/ съел/ съела/ всё, что было на
тарелке. (m/f)
Tui/ syehl/ sYEHlah/ fsyaw, shtaw
bUIlah nah tahrYEHlkyih.

You have eaten everything
on your plate.

Можешь поиграть после ужина.
MAWzhihsh paheegrAHt' pAWslih
OOzheenah.

You can play after dinner.

Приятного аппетита!
PreeYAHtnahvah ahpihtEEtah!

Enjoy your meal!

(Всё) было вкусно! Очень вкусно.
(Fsyaw) bUIlah fkOOsnah! AWchihn'
fkOOsnah!

That (Everything) was
delicious!

/Обед/ Ужин/ был очень вкусный.
/AhbYEHt/ OOzheen/ buil AWchihn'/
fkOOsnuiy.

/Lunch/ Dinner/ was
delicious.

Всё! Можно мне выйти из-за стола?
Fsyaw! MAWzhnah mnYEH vuiytEE
eez-zah stahlAH?

All gone! May I leave the
table?

A friend in need is a friend indeed.

Друзья познаются в беде

Разговор   Conversation

These are the pages you use to enlist, explain, persuade, coax, and insist when speaking with your child. When all else fails, there is always, Потому что я так сказал/-а. ("Because I say so!") – appropriate justification in any language.

Что это? Какой шум!   What is that? What a noise!
Shtaw EHtah? KahkOY shoom!

Что ты слышишь?   What do you hear?
Shtaw tui slUIsheesh?

Я тебя напугал/-а? (m/f)   Did I frighten you?
Yah tihbYAH nahpoogAHl/-ah?

Могу я чем-нибудь помочь?   Is there anything I can do?
MahgOO yah chYEHm-neeboot'pahmAWch'?

Что ты говоришь?   What are you saying?
Shtaw tui gahvahrEEsh?

34

Думай, прежде чем говоришь.　Think before you speak.
DOOmahy, prYEHzhdyih chyehm
gahvahrEEsh.

Что ты сказал/-a? (m/f)　What did you say?
Shtaw tui skahzAHl/-ah?

Я слушаю.　I'm listening.
Yah slOOshahyoo.

Как ты красиво поёшь!　How beautifully you sing!
Kahk tui krahsEEvah pahYAWsh!

Какой /ая ты разговорчивый/-ая! (m/f)　How talkative you are!
/KahkOY/ KahkAHyah/ tui rahzgah-
vAWrcheevuiy/-vahyah!

Ну-ка сиди прямо.　(Command)　Come on!　Sit up straight.
NOO-kah seedEE prYAHmah.

Сядь ко мне на колени.　(Invitation)　Sit on my lap.
Syaht' kah mnYEH nah kahlYEHnee.

Подними голову.　Raise your head.
PahdneemEE gAWlahvoo.

Возьми. Не бери...　Take it.　Don't take...
Vahz'mEE. Nih bihrEE...

Где погремушка?　Where is the rattle?
Gdyeh pahgrihmOOshkah?

/Держи/ Возьми/ погремушку.　/Hold/ Take/ the rattle.
/DihrzhEE/ Vahz'mEE/ pahgrihmOOshkoo.

Отпусти (меня)!　Let (me) go!
AhtpoostEE (mnYAH) !

На что ты смотришь?　What are you looking at?
Nah shtaw tui smAWtreesh?

Я ищу...
Yah eeschOO...

I'm looking for...

О чём ты думаешь?
Ah chyawm tui dOOmahihsh?

What are you thinking about?

Чему ты улыбаешься?
ChihmOO tui ooluibAHihshsah?

What are you smiling at?

Я вижу, что ты мечтаешь.
Yah vEEzhoo, shtaw tui mihchtAHyish.

I can see you're dreaming.

Покажи мне, как ты двигаешь руками!
PahkahzhEE mnYEH, kahk tui dvEEgahihsh rookAHmee!

Show me how you move your arms!

Кто/ я/ он/ она/ это/?
Ktaw/ yah/ awn/ ahnAH/ EHtah/?

Who/ am I/ is he/ is she/ is it/?

Я тебя знаю.
Yah tihbYAH znAHyoo.

I know you.

Это/ твой брат/ твоя сестра/.
EHTah/ tvoy braht/ tvahYAH sihstrAH/.

It's/ your brother/ your sister/.

Он/ маленький/ большой/.
Awn/ mAHlihn'keey/ bahl'shOY/.

He is/ small/ large/.

Она/ маленькая/ большая/.
AhnAH/ mAHlihn'kahyah/ bahl'shAHyah/.

She is/ small/ large/.

Оно/ маленькое/ большое/.
AhnAW/ mAHlihn'kahyih/ bahl'shAWyih/.

It is/ small/ large/.

У тебя глаза совсем как у твоего отца.
Oo tihbYAH glahzAH sahfsYEHm kahk oo tvahyihvAW ahtsAH.

You have eyes just like your father's.

Улыбнись, пожалуйста!
OoluibnEEs', pahzhAHloostah!

Please, smile!

Я хочу тебя сфотографировать.
Yah khahchOO tihbYAH sfahtah-
grahfEErahvaht'.

I want to take your picture.

Сделай приятную улыбку!
ZdYEHlahy preeYAHtnooyoo
oolUIpkoo!

Show me a nice smile!

Какой длинный рассказ!
KahkOY dlEEnnuiy rahskAHs!

What a long story!

Тебе нравится, не правда ли!
TihbYEH nrAHveetsah, nih
prAHvdah lee!

You like that, don't you!

Давай я потру тебе животик.
DahvAHy yah pahtrOO tihbYEH
zheevAWteek.

Let me rub your tummy.

Куда ты идёшь?
KoodAH tui eedYAWsh?

Where are you going?

Посмотри на...
PahsmahtrEE nah....

Look at.....

Ты видишь...?
Tui vEEdeesh ...?

Do you see...?

Повернись кругом.
PahvihrnEEs' kroogAWm.

Turn around.

Ты можешь держать мышь?
Tui mAWzhihsh dihrzhAHt' muish?

Can you hold the mouse?

Что у тебя во рту?
Shtaw oo tihbYAH vah-rtOO?

What do you have in your
mouth?

Тебе нельзя это брать в рот.
TihbYEH nihl'zYAH EHtah braht'
vrawt.

You cannot put that in your
mouth.

37

Не/ ударяй/ плескайся/ кусайся/ плачь/!
Nih/ oodahrYAHy/ plihskAHysah/
koosAHysah/ plahch'/!

No/ kicking/ splashing/
biting/ crying/!

Не ударяй меня ногой!
Nih oodahrYAHy mnYAH nahgOY!

Don't kick me!

Как ты ударяешь ногой!
Kahk tui oodahrYAHihsh nahgOY!

How you kick!

Ты мочишь меня водой!
Tui mAWcheesh mnYAH vahdOY!

You're getting me wet!

Не плачь. Почему ты плачешь?
Nih plahch'. PahchihmOO tui
plAHchihsh?

Don't cry. Why are you
crying?

Я плачу, потому что...
Yah plAHchoo, pahtahmOO shtaw...

I'm crying because...

Я слышал/-а, как ты плачешь. (m/f)
Yah slUIshahl/-ah, kahk tui
plAHchihsh.

I heard you crying.

Где кубики?
Gdyeh kOObeekee?

Where are the blocks?

Достань кубик.
DahstAHn' kOObeek.

Reach for the block.

Хочешь поиграть в мяч?
KhAWchihsh paheegrAHt' fmyahch?

Would you like to play
with the ball?

Мы идём в гости к бабушке.
Mui eedYAWm fgAWstee kbAH-
booshkyih.

We're going to visit
Grandma.

Собирайся. Я собираюсь.
SahbeerAHysah. Yah sahbeerAHyoos'.

Get ready. I'm getting ready.

Я уже/ готов/ готова/: (m/f)
Yah oozhYEH/ gahtAWf/ gahtAWvah:

I'm ready:

уходить, итти гулять,
ookhahdEET',eeTEE goolYAHt',

to leave, to go for a walk,

есть (or) кушать.
yehst' (or) kOOshaht'. (more polite)

to eat.

Мы покажем ей, как ты быстро растёшь.
Mui pahkAHzhihm yehy, kahk tui
bUIstrah rahstYAWsh.

We'll show her how fast
you're growing.

Иди сюда (к маме).
EedEE syoodAH (k'mAHmyih).

Come here (to mommy).

Иди ко мне.
EedEE kah mnYEH.

Come to me.

Смотри, как ты идёшь!
SmahtrEE, kahk tui eedYAWsh!

Look how you go!
(walk)

Давай посмотрим, как ты умеешь ходить.
DahvAHy pahsmAWtreem, kahk tui
oomYEHihsh khahdEEt'.

Let's see how you walk.

Посмотри-ка на эти зубы!
PahsmahtrEE-kah nah EHtee zOObui!

Look at those teeth!

У тебя болят зубы ?
Oo tihbYAH bahlYAHt zOObui ?

Do your teeth hurt?

Барабань в барабан!
BahrahbAHn' fbahrahbAHn!

Bang the drum!

Маршируй под музыку!
MahrsheerOOy pawt mOOzuikoo!

March to the music!

Позвони в бубенчик!
PahzvahnEE fboobYEHncheek!

Ring the bell!

39

Какая красивая музыка!
KahkAHyah krahsEEvahyah
mOOzuikah!

What beautiful music!

Хлопай в ладоши!
KhlAWpahy vlahdAWshee!

Clap your hands!

Сыграй другую песню!
SuigrAHy droogOOyoo pYEHsnyoo!

Play another song!

Вот ребёнок, такой же как ты.
Vawt rihbYAWnahk, tahkOY zheh
kahk tui.

Here is a baby like you.

Кто это в зеркале?
Ktaw EHtah fzYEHrkahlyih?

Who is that in the mirror?

Где у ребёнка/ ножки/ глазки/?
Gdyeh oo rihbYAWNkah/ nAWzhkee/
glAHskee/?

Where are baby's/ feet/
eyes/?

Вот/ твой носик, ротик/ твоё ушко/.
Vawt/ tvoy nAWseek, rAWteek/
tvahYAW OOshkah/.

Here is/ your nose, mouth/
ear/.

Давай прогуляемся в детской коляске.
DahvAHy prahgoolYAHihmsah
fdYEHtskoy kahlYAHskyih.

Let's go for a stroll in your
carriage.

Нам нужно идти к врачу.
Nahm nOOzhnah eetEE kvrahchOO.

We have to go to the
doctor.

Не бойся. Ничего страшного.
Nih bOYsah. NeechihvAW strAHshnahvah.

Don't be afraid. It's O.K.

Ты боишься?
Tui bahEEshsah?

Are you afraid?

Я не боюсь.
Yah nih bahYOOs'.

I'm not afraid.

Я иду за тобой!
Yah eedOO zah tahbOY!

I'm coming to get you!

Поймал/-а! (m/f)
PahymAHl/-ah!

Got-Cha!

Тебе нравится...(что-то)?
TihbYEH nrAHveetsah...(shtaw-tah)?

Do you like...(something)?

Разве ты не хочешь...+ infinitive?
RAHzvyih tui nih khAWchihsh.... ?

Don't you want to... + infinitive?

Разве ты не хочешь... + noun?
RAHzvyih tui nih khAWchihsh.... ?

Don't you want... + noun?

Пойдём немного погуляем.
PahydYAWm nihmnAWgah pahgoo-lYAHihm.

Let's take a little walk.

Держись за мою руку.
DihrzhEEs' zah mahYOO rOOkoo.

Take my hand.

Сядь на свой стул.
Syaht' nah svoy stool.

Sit on your chair.

Не залезай на стул.
Nih zahlihZAHy nah stool.

Don't climb up on the chair.

Смотри: ступенька.
SmahtrEE: stoopYEHn'kah.

Watch the step.

Поднимись по лестнице.
PahdneemEEs' pah lYEHstneetsih.

Climb the stairs.

Спускайся осторожно по лестнице.
SpooskAHysah ahstahrAWzhnah pah lYEHstneetsih.

Come down the stairs carefully.

Держись за перила.
DihrzhEEs' zah pihrEElah.

Hold on to the bannister.

41

Засунь ногу в штанину.
ZahsOOn' nAWgoo fshtahnEEnoo.

Put your foot in the pants.

Вынь руку из рукава.
Vuin' rOOkoo eez rookahvAH.

Pull your arm out of the sleeve.

Папа поможет тебе надеть пижаму.
PAHpah pahmAWzhiht tihbYEH nahdYEHt' peezhAHmoo.

Daddy will help put on your pajamas.

Сходи и принеси свои новые туфли.
S'khahdEE ee preenihsEE svahEE nAW-vuiyih tOOflee.

Go and get your new shoes.

Что у тебя в/ руке/ кармане/?
Shtaw oo tihbYAH v/ rookYEH/ kahrmAHnyih/?

What do you have in your /hand/ pocket/?

Дай/ его/ её/ его/ мне. (m/f/n/)
Dahy/ yihvAW/ yihYAW/ yihvAW/ mnYEH.

Give it to me.

Не трогай это. Это грязное.
Nih trAWgahy EHtah. EHtah gryahznahYEH.

Don't touch it. It's dirty.

Иди и возьми/ кубики / мяч/.
EedEE ee vahz'mEE/ kOObeekee/ myahch/.

Go and get the/ blocks/ ball/.

Не сломай. * Не разбей.**
Nih slahmAHy. Nih rahzbYEHy.

Don't break it. (toy)* (cup)**

Не вставай. Сиди.
Nih fstahvAHy. SeedEE.

Don't get up. Stay seated.

Позаботься о мишке.
PahzahbAWt'sah aw mEEshkyih.

Take care of teddy.

Дай/ ему/ ей/ чашку чая.
Dahy/ yihmOO/ yehy/ chAHshkoo chAHyih.

Give/ him/ her/ a cup of tea.

Погладь собаку ласково.
PahglAHt' sahbAHkoo lAHskahvah.

Pet the dog gently.

Не/ ударяй ногой/ ударяй/!
Nih/oodahrYAHy nahgOY/oodahrYAHy/!

Stop/ kicking/ hitting/!

Не/ кусайся/ плачь/!
Nih/ koosAHysah/ plahch'/!

Stop/ biting/ crying/!

Остановись! Стой!
AhstahnahvEEs'! Stoy!

Stop!

Вон отсюда! / Прочь! / Уходи!
Vawn ahtsYOOdah! / Prawch'!
OokhahdEE!

Get out of here!
Go away!

Мне так больно.
MnYEH tahk bAWl'nah.

That hurts (me).
(physical)

(Не) заходи.
(Nih) zahkhahdEE.

(Don't) go in.

Дай мне твою руку
Dahy mnYEH tvahYOO rOOkoo.

Give me your hand.

Ты очень шумишь!
Tui AWchihn' shoomEEsh!

You're making a lot of noise!

Кто кричит?
Ktaw kreechEET?

Who's shouting?

Не кричи/ в доме/ в этой комнате/.
Nih kreechEE/ fdAWmyih/ vYEHtoy kAWmnahtyih/.

Don't shout/in the house/ in this room/.

Тише! (or) Тихо!
TEEshih! (or) TEEkhah!

Be quiet!

Я сейчас занят/-а. (m/f)
Yah sihchAHs /zAHnyiht/ zahnyihtAH/.

I'm busy now.

Я спешу. Поторопись!
Yah spihshOO. PahtahrahpEEs'!

I'm in a hurry. Hurry!

У меня нет времени.
Oo mnYAH nyeht vrYEHmihnee.

I have no time.

/Нам/ Мне/ надо идти (уходить).
/Nahm/ MnYEH/ nAHdah eetEE
(ookhahdeet').

/We/ I/ must go (leave).

Я скоро вернусь.
Yah skAWrah vihrnOOs'.

I'll come back soon.

Подожди! (меня)
PahdahzhdEE! (mnYAH)

Wait! (for me)

Я подожду тебя.
Yah pahdahzhdOO tihbYAH.

I'll wait for you.

Я тебя жду!
Yah tihbYAH zhdoo!

I'm waiting for you!

Оставайся там.
AhstahvAHysah tahm.

Stay there.

Не двигайся с места.
Nih dvEEgahysah smYEHstah.

Don't move from that spot.

Не двигай (рукой).
Nih dvEEgahy (rookOY).

Don't move (your hand).

Мне бы хотелось, чтобы ты остался/ (m)
осталась /(f):
MnYEH bui khahtYEHlahs', shTAWbui
tui ahstAHlsah/ ahstAHlahs'/:

I would like you to stay:

в детской коляске,
fdYEHtskoy kahlYAHskyih,

in the carriage,

на кухне.
nah kOOkhnyih.

in the kitchen.

Я хочу, чтобы ты/ остался (m)/ осталась
(f)/ в своей комнате.
Yah khahchOO, shtAWbui tui /ah-
stAHlsah/ ahstAHlahs / fsvahYEHy
kAWmnahtyih.

I want you to stay in your
room.

Подожди минуту, пожалуйста.
PahdahzhdEE meenOOtoo, pahzhAHL-
oostah.

Just a moment, please.

(Не) уходи.
(Nih) ookhahdEE.

(Don't) go away.

Уходи оттуда.
OokhahDEE ahtTOOdah.

Come away from there.

Перестань (так делать).
PihrihstAHn' (tahk dYEHlaht').

Stop doing that.

Делай, что я тебе говорю!
DYEHlahy, shtaw yah tihbYEH
gahvahrYOO!

Do what I tell you!

Я же тебе говорил/-а! (m/f)
Yah zheh tihbYEH gahvahrEEL/-ah!

What did I tell you!

Делай так, как тебе сказано!
DYEHlahy tahk, kahk tihbYEH
skAHzahnah!

Do as you are told!

Ты/ должен был/(m) /должна была/ (f)
сказать мне об этом.
Tui/ dAWLzhihn buil/ dahlzhnAH builAH/
skahzAHt' mnYEH ahb EHtahm.

You should have told me
about this.

Я с тобой говорю!
Yah stahbOY gahvahrYOO!

I'm speaking to you!

С кем ты говоришь?
Skyehm tui gahvahrEEsh?

To whom are you speak-
ing?

Что ты хочешь, чтобы я сделал/-а? (m/f)/
Shtaw tui khAWchihsh, shtAWbui yah/
zdYEHlahl/-ah/?

What do you want me to do?

Не причиняй мне беспокойство.
Nih preecheenYAHy mnYEH bihspah-
kOYstvah.

Don't give me trouble.

Не мешай мне сейчас.
Nih mihshAHy mnYEH sihchAHs.

Don't disturb me now.

Не дерись! (s) Зачем вы спорите? (pl)
Nih dihrEEs'! ZahchYEHm vui spAWr-
eetyih?

Don't fight! Why argue?

О чём у тебя идёт спор?
Ah chyawm oo tihbYAH eedYAWt spawr?

What's the argument about?

Давай(те) по очереди. (s/pl)
DahvAHy(tyih) pah AWchyehrihdee.

Take turns.

Не беспокой/ его/ её/.
Nih bihspahkOY/ yihvAW/ yihYAW/.

Don't bother/ him/ her/.

Не беспокой кошку.
Nih bihspahkOY kAWshkoo.

Don't bother the cat.

Не дразни его.
Nih drahznEE yihvAW.

Don't tease him.

Не обращай на/ него/ неё/ внимания.
Nih ahbrahschAHy nah/ nyihvAW/
nihYAW/ vneemAHneeyih.

Don't pay any attention to / him/ her/.

Оставь/ его/ её/ его/ (m/f/n/) в покое.
AhstAHf'/ yihvAW/ yihYAW/ yihvAW/
fpahkAWyih.

Leave/ him/ her/ it/ alone.

Отстань от меня!
AhtstAHn' awt mnYAH!

Leave me alone!

Не подбирай это.
Nih pahdbeerAHy EHtah.

Don't pick that up.

/Открой/ Закрой/ дверь.
/AhtKkrOY/ ZahkrOY/ dvyehr'.

/Open/ Close/ the door.

Запри дверь (на замок).
ZahprEE dvyehr' (nah zahmAWk).

Lock the door.

Не открывай окно.
Nih ahtkruivAHy ahknAW.

Don't open the window.

Ты/ закрыл/-а /дверь/ окно/? (m/f)
Tui/ zahkrUll/-ah/ dvyehr'/ ahknAW/?

Did you close the/ door/ window/?

Не ложись на подоконник.
Nih lahzhEEs' nah pahdahkAWnneek.

Don't lean on the window sill.

Положи коробку вон туда.
PahlahzhEE kahrAWpkoo vawn toodAH.

Put the box over there.

(Не) прыгай!
(Nih) prUIgahy!

(Don't) jump!

Медленно!
MYEHdlihnnah!

Slowly!

Не беги. Иди медленнее.
Nih bihgEE. EedEE mYEHdlihnihyih.

Don't run. Go slower.

Иди как можно медленней.
EedEE kahk mAWzhnah mYEHdlihn-nyehy.

Walk as slowly as possible.

Ты оступишься.
Tui ahstOOpeeshsah.

You'll trip.

Быстрее! Не спеши!
BuistrYEHyih! Nih spihshEE!

Hurry up!
Don't hurry!

Нам нужно спешить.
Nahm nOOzhnah spihshEEt'.

We must hurry.

/Поставь/ Положи/ туфли на место.
/PahstAHf'/ PahlahzhEE/ tOOflee
nah mYEHstah.

Put the shoes back in
their place.

Не пиши на стене.
Nih peeshEE nah stihnYEH.

Don't write on the wall.

Что это лежит/ на столе/ на полу/?
Shtaw EHtah lihzhEEt/ nah stahlYEH/
nah pahlOO/?

What is that lying on the
/table/ floor/?

/Отойди на шаг/ Подойди на шаг/.
/AhtahydEE nah shahk/ PahdahydEE/
nah shahk/.

Step/ back/ forward/.

Не трогай плиту.
Nih trAWgahy plEEtoo.

Don't touch the range.

Ты обожжёшься!
Tui ahbahzhzhYAWshsah!

You will burn yourself!

Ты/ обжёгся/ обожглась/? (m/f)
Tui/ ahbzhYAWksah/ ahbahzhglAHs'/?

Did you burn yourself?

Не играй со спичками!
Nih eegrAHy sah spEEchkahmee!

Don't play with matches!

Не зажигай спичку.
Nih zahzheegAHy spEEchkoo.

Don't light the match.

Держись подальше от лестницы,
барбекю, улицы.
DihrzhEES' pahdAHl'shih awt
lYEHstneetsui, bahrbihkYOO, OOleetsui.

Stay (Stand) away from
the stairs, barbecue, street.

Не перебегай через улицу!
Nih pihrihbihgAHy chYEHrihs
OOleetsoo!

Don't run across the street!

48

Держись за детскую коляску.
DihrzhEEs' zah dYEHtskooyoo
kahlYAHskoo.

Hold on to the carriage.

Посмотри/ налево/ направо/ перед тем,
как переходить улицу.
PahsmahtrEE/ nahlYEHvah/ nah-
prAHvah/ pYEHrihd tyehm, kahk
pihrihkhahdEEt' OOleetsoo.

Look /left/ right/ before
crossing the street.

Подожди, когда зажжётся зелёный свет.
PahdahzhdEE, kahgdAH zahzhYAWtsah
zihlYAWnuiy svyeht.

Wait for the green light.

Впредь будь/ осторожен/ осторожна/!
Fpryeht' boot'/ ahstahrAWzhihn/ ahstahrAWzhnah! (m/f)

From now on, be careful!

Держи/ его/ её/ его/ на ручке/ обеими
руками. (m/f/n)
DihrzhEE/ yihvAW/ yihYAW/ yihvAW/
nah rOOchkyih/ ahbYEHeemee
rookAHmee.

Hold it/ by the handle/
with both hands/.

Обращай внимание на то, что ты
делаешь.
AhbrahschAHy fneemAHneeyih
nah taw, shtaw tui dYEHlahihsh.

Pay attention to what you
are doing.

Не урони/ его/ её/ его/ на землю. (m/f/n)
Nih oorahnEE/ yihvAW/ yihYAW/
yihvAW/ nah zYEHmlyoo.

Don't drop it on the ground.

Что ты/ с ним/ с ней/ сделал/-а? (m/f)
Shtaw tui/ sneem/ snyehy/ zdYEHl-
ahl/-ah?

What did you do to it?

Не порежь палец. Нож острый.
Nih pahrYEHzh' pAHLihts. Nawzh
AWstruiy.

Don't cut your finger.
The knife is sharp.

Не хватай это.
Nih khvahtAHy EHtah.

Don't grab that.

Как ты думаешь?
Kahk tui dOOmahihsh?

What do you think?

...,потому что я так сказал/-а. (m/f)
...,pahtahmOO shtaw yah tahk skahzAHl/-ah.

...because I say so

...,потому что это так.
...,pahtahmOO shtaw EHtah tahk.

...because that's the way it is.

Из-за тебя...
Eez-zah tihbYAH...

Because of you...

Ты думаешь что...?
Tui dOOmahihsh shtaw...?

Do you think that...?

У меня (к тебе) большая просьба.
Oo mnYAH (ktihbYEH) bahl'shAHyih prAWs'bah.

I have a favor to ask (of you).

Не/ мог/ могла/ бы ты....? (m/f)
Nih/ mawk/ mahglAH/ bui tui...?

Could you...?

Принеси, пожалуйста, швабру.
PreenihsEE, pahzhAHloostah, shvAHbroo.

Please bring me the mop.

Ты не/ мог/ могла/ бы помочь мне
приготовить обед? (m/f)
Tui nih/ mawk/ mahglAH/ bui pahmAWch' mnYEH preegahtAWveet' ahbYEHt?

Can you help me fix lunch?

Ты не/ мог/ могла/ бы отнести это блюдо?
Tui nih/ mawk/ mahglAH/ bui ahtnihstEE EHtah blYOOdah? (m/f)

Can you carry the dish?

Ты бросил/-а камень? (m/f)
Tui brAWseel/-ah kAHmihn'?

Did you throw the stone?

Я/ видел/-а, как ты это сделал/-а. (m/f)
Yah/ vEEdihl/-ah, kahk tui EHtah
zdYEHlahl/-ah. (m/f)

I saw you do this.

Могу ли я спросить тебя....?
MahgOO lee yah sprahsEEt' tihbYAH...?

May I ask you.........?

Скажи брату, чтобы он пришёл наверх.
SkahzhEE brAHtoo, shtAWbui awn
preeshYAWl nahvYEHrkh.

Tell your brother to come
upstairs.

Скажи сестре, что я её ищу.
SkahzhEE sihstrYEH, shtaw yah
yihYAW eeschOO.

Tell your sister I'm looking for her.

Поговори/ с ним/ с ней/ по-хорошему.
PahgahvahrEE/ sneem/ snyehy/ pah-khah-
rAWshihmoo.

Speak to/ him/ her/ nicely.

Пусть/ он/ она/ скажет мне, что/ он/
она/ хочет.
Poost'/ awn/ ahnAH/ skAHzhiht mnYEH,
shtaw/ awn/ ahnAH/ khAWchiht.

Let/ him/ her/ tell me what
/ he/ she/ wants.

Скажи ему, что ему нужно придти.
SkahzhEE ihmOO, shtaw ihmOO
nOOzhnah preetEE.

Tell him he should come.

Твоя сестра должна войти.
TvahYAH sihstrAH dahlzhnAH
vahytEE.

Your sister should come
in.

Я хочу/ его/ её/ видеть.
Yah khahchOO/ yihvAW/ yihYAW/
vEEdiht'.

I want to see/ him/ her/.

У тебя грязная рубашка.
Oo tihbYAH grYAHznahyah roobAHshkah.

Your shirt is dirty.

Иди в свою комнату и надень другую рубашку.
EedEE fsvahYOO kAWMnahtoo ee nahdYEHn' droogOOyoo roobAHshkoo.

Go to your room, and put on another shirt.

Покажи мне, где твоя комната.
PahkahzhEE mnYEH, gdyeh tvahYAH kAWmnahtah.

Show me where your room is.

Что ты делаешь?
Shtaw tui dYEHlahihsh?

What are you doing?

Ходи на цыпочках, когда ребёнок спит.
KhahdEE nah tsUIpahchkahk, kahgdAH rihbYAWnahk speet.

Tiptoe when baby is sleeping.

Ты можешь убаюкать ребёнка?
Tui mAWzhihsh oobahYOOkaht' rihbYAWnkah?

Can you rock the baby?

Не пугай/ его/ её/.
Nih poogAHy/ yihvAW/ yihYAW/.

Don't scare/ him/ her/.

Сиди. Стой.
SeedEE. Stoy.

Remain/ seated/ standing/.

/Сидите/ Встаньте/: (pl)
/SeedEEtyih/ FstAHn'tyih/:

/Sit/ Stand/: (pl)

/поближе друг к другу/,
/pahblEEzhih drook kdrOOgoo/,

/a little closer to each other/,

/подальше друг от друга/.
/pahdAHl'shih drook awt drOOgah/.

/a little further from each other/.

Ты это сделал/-a? (назло)   (m/f)
Tui EHtah zdYEHlahl/-ah (nahzlAW)?

Did you do it? (out of spite)

Сделай по-моему.
ZdYEHlahy pah-mAWihmoo.

Do it the way I want. (Do it my way.)

Я хочу, чтобы ты мне сказал/-а правду.
Yah khahchOO, shtAWbui tui mnYEH
skahZAHL/-ah PRAHVdoo. (m/f)

I want you to tell me the truth.

Посмотри мне прямо в глаза.
PahsmahTREE mnYEH prYAHmah
fglahzAH.

Look me straight in the eye.

Я хочу тебе кое-что сказать.
Yah khahchOO tihbYEH kahyihshtAW
skahzAHt'.

I want to tell you something.

Расскажи мне об этом.
RahskahzhEE mnYEH ahb EHtahm.

Tell me about it.

Говори/ медленнее/ яснее/.
GahvahrEE/ mYEHdlihnihyih/
yihsnYEHyih/.

Speak more/ slowly/ clearly/.

Говори как можно тише.
GahvahrEE kahk mAWzhnah tEEshih.

Speak as softly as possible.

Послушай внимательно.
PahslOOshahy fneemAHtyihl'nah.

Listen carefully.

Послушай, что я хочу тебе сказать.
PahslOOshahy, shtaw yah khahchOO
tihbYEH skahzAHt'.

Listen to what I have to say.

Что с тобой сегодня?
Shtaw stahbOY sihvAWdnyih?

What's with you today?

Со мной ничего.
SahmnOY neechihvAW.

Nothing's with me.

Ты (сегодня) в/ плохом/ хорошем/
настроении.
Tui (sihvAWdnyih) f/ plahkhAWm/
khahrAWshihm/ nahstrahYEHneeee.

You are in / bad/ good/ mood (today).

53

Обещай хорошо себя вести! AhbihschAHy khahrahshAW sihbYAH vehstEE!	Promise to be good!
Я обещаю. Я бы не хотел/-а. (m/f) Yah ahbihschAHyoo. Yah bui nih khahtYEHl/-ah.	I promise. I'd rather not.
Я надеюсь, что ты будешь хорошо себя вести. Yah nahdYEHyoos', shtaw tui bOOdihsh khahrahshAW sihbYAH vihstEE.	I expect you to be good.
Веди себя хорошо,... VihdEE sihbYAH khahrahshAW,...	Behave yourself,...
...а то ты у меня (награды) не получишь! ...ah taw tui oo mnYAH (nahgrAHdui) nih pahlOOcheesh!	...or you won't get any (reward)!
Ты понимаешь, о чём я говорю? Tui pahneemAHyihsh, ah chawm yah gahvahrYOO?	Do you understand what I'm saying?
Я думаю, что я понимаю,о чём ты говоришь. Yah dOOmahyoo, shtaw yah pahneemAH- yoo, ah chawm tui gahvahrEEsh.	I think I understand what you're saying.
Не выходи из себя. Nih vuikhahdEE ees sihbYAH.	Don't lose your temper.
Понимаешь? PahneemAHyihsh?	Do you understand?
Будь послушным. Boot' pahslOOshnuim.	Don't be naughty.
Как ты упрям/-а! (m/f) Kahk tui ooprYAHm/-ah!	Are you stubborn!

Не испытывай моё терпение!
Nih eespUIt'uivahy mahYAW tihr-
pYEHneeyih!

Don't try my patience!

Не нервничай.
Nih nYEHrvneechahy.

Don't be nervous.

Успокойся.
OospahkOYsah.

Calm down.

Всё будет в порядке.
Fsyaw bOOdiht fparYAHdkyih.

Everything will be all right.

Покажи мне, где у тебя болит.
PahkahzhEE mnYEH, gdyeh oo tihbYAH bahlEET.

Show me where it hurts.

Ты упал/-а. (m/f)
Tui oopAHl/-ah/.

You fell.

Ты/ ударился/ ударилась/ головой. (m/f)
Tui/ oodAHreelsah/ oodAHeelahs'/ gahlahvOY.

You have bumped your head.

Потри рукой.
PahtrEE rookOY.

Rub it with your hand.

Открой рот.
AhtkrOY rawt.

Open your mouth.

Не клади камешки в рот.
Nih klahdEE kAHmehshkee vrawt.

Don't put the pebble in your mouth.

Перестань строить рожи!
PihrihstAHn' strOYeet' rAWzhee!

Stop making faces!

Тебе же лучше будет.
TihbYEH zheh lOOchih bOOdiht.

That will do you good.

Вытри свой нос.
VUItree svoy naws.

Wipe your nose.

Дыши через нос.
DuishEE chYEHrihs naws.

Breathe through your nose.

Не говори мне, что...
Nih gahvahrEE mnYEH, shtaw...

Don't tell me that...

Забудь о своей игрушке на мгновение.
ZahbOOT' ah svahYEHy eegrOOshkyih
nah mgnahvYEHneeyih.

Forget your toy for a
moment.

У тебя уже их много.
Oo tihbYAH oozhYEH eekh mnAWgah.

You already have lots of
them.

Играй со своими игрушками.
EegrAHy sah svahEEmee eegrOOshkahmee.

Play with your own toys.

Не трогай мои игрушки.
Nih trAWgahy mahEE eegrOOshkee.

Don't touch my toys.

Я хочу всё!
Yah khahchOO fsyaw!

I want them all!

Не забудь (принести) цветные карандаши.
Nih zahbOOT' (preenihstEE) svyeht-
nUIyih kahrahndahshEE.

Don't forget (to bring) your
crayons.

Иди со мной.
EedEE sahmnoy.

Come with me.

Немедленно!
NihmYEHdlihnnah!

Immediately!

Пойди первым.
PahydEE pYEHrvuim.

You go first.

Сюда. Иди за мной!
SyoodAH. EedEE zah mnoy!

This way. Follow me!

Ты думаешь, что ты можешь так сделать?
Tui dOOmahihsh, shtaw tui mAWzhihsh
tahk zdYEHlaht'?

Do you think that you can
do it?

Ты можешь так сделать?
Tui mAWzhihsh tahk zdYEHlaht'?

Can you do that?

Разве ты не можешь так сделать?
RAHSvih tui nih mAWzhihsh tahk
zdYEHlaht'?

Can't you do that?

Иди/ наверх/ вниз/ помогать бабушке.
EedEE/ nahvYEHrkh fnees/
pahmahgAHt' bAHbooshkyih.

Go/ upstairs /downstairs
/and help Grandma.

Играй/ наверху/ внизу/.
EegrAHy/ nahvihrkhOO/ fneezOO/.

Play/ upstairs/ downstairs/.

Играй на тротуаре.
EegrAHy nah trahtooAHryih.

Play on the sidewalk

Иди на улицу. Войди в дом.
EedEE nah OOleetsoo. VahydEE fdawm.

Go outside.
Come inside.

/Включи/ Потуши/ свет.
/FklyoochEE/ PahtooshEE/ svyeht.

Turn on/ Turn out/ the
light.

Зажги лампу.
ZahzhgEE lAHmpoo.

Light the lamp.

Поставь видиокассету.
PahstAHf' veedeeahkahsYEHtyoo.

Put on the video.

Я не могу найти дорогу в темноте.
Yah nih mahgOO nahytEE dahrAWgoo
ftihmnahtYEH.

I can't find the way the
in dark.

Это твоё?
EHtah tvahYAW?

Is this yours?

Это (не) твоё.
EHtah (nih) tvahYAW.

This is (not) yours.

Это моё? Это (не) моё.
EHtah mahYAW? EHtah (nih) mahYAW.

Is this mine?
This is (not) mine.

Тебе не разрешено кушать в гостиной.
TihbYEH nih rahzrihshihnAW kOOshaht'
fgahstEEnoy.

You are not allowed to
eat in the living room.

Ешь (Кушай) на кухне,
Yehsh (kOOshahy) nah kOOkhnyih,

Eat in the kitchen,

...чтобы не запачкать ковёр.
...shTAWbui nih zahpAHchkaht'
kahvYAWr.

...so you don't stain
the rug.

Не спрашивай/ так часто/ больше/!
Nih sprAHsheevahy/ tahk chAHstah/
bAWl'shih/!

Don't ask /so often/ again/!

Не давай мне...
Nih dahvAHy mnYEH...

Don't give me...

Подожди, пока я приду.
PahdahzhdEE, pahkAH yah preedOO.

Wait until I come back.

(Потом) мы поговорим.
(PahtAWMm mui pahgahvahrEEm.

(Then) we'll talk.

Делай, что (ты) хочешь.
DYEHlahy, shtaw (tui) khAWchihsh.

Do what you like.

Ты отвечаешь за своего маленького брата.
Tui ahtvihchAHihsh zah svahyihvAW
mAHlihn'kahvah brAHtah.

You're responsible for
your brother.

Кто отвечает за...?
Ktaw ahtvihchAHiht zah...?

Who is responsible for...?

Слушайся меня!
SlOOshahysah mnYAH!

Obey me!

Иди в свою комнату!
EedEE fsvahYOO kAWmnahtoo!

Go to your room!

Я был/-а у себя в комнате. (m/f)
Yah buil/-AH oo sihbYAH fkAWmnahtyih.

I was in my room.

Не ссорьтесь друг с другом.
Nih sAWr'tihs' drook sdrOOgahm.

Don't quarrel with one another.

Закрой холодильник.
ZahkrOY khahlahdEEl'neek.

Close the refrigerator.

Поставь масло в холодильник.
PahstAHf' mAHslah fkhahlahdEEl'neek.

Put the butter in the refrigerator.

Не торопись.
Nih tahrahpEEs'.

Take your time.

Вытри туфли о половик.
VUItree tOOflee ah pahlahvEEk.

Wipe your shoes on the mat.

Сними свои туфли.
SneemEE svahEE tOOflee.

Remove your shoes.

Не ходи босиком!
Nih khahdEE bahseekAWm!

Don't walk barefoot!

Что поделаешь?
Shtaw pahdYEHlahihsh?

What can we do?
(Seemingly nothing)

Что бы нам поделать?
Shtaw bui nahm pahdYEHlaht'?

What can we do?
(Activity with child)

Что мы можем сделать?
Shtaw mui mAWzhihm zdYEHlaht'?

What can we do?
(Offering help)

Давай попробуем вместе.
DahvAHy pahprAWbooihm vmYEHstyih.

Let's try together.

Скажи мне, что (с тобой) случилось.
SkahzhEE mnYEH, shtaw (stahbOY) sloochEElahs'.

Tell me what happened (to you).

Вот как это случилось.
Vawt kahk EHtah sloochEElahs'.

It happened this way.

Не выражайся!
Nih vuirahzhAHysah!

Do not use bad language! (Swearing)

Ты всегда огрызаешься!
Tui fsyegdAH ahgruizAHyihshsah!

You have an answer for everything!

Я жду ответа.
Yah zhdoo ahtvYEHtah.

I'm waiting for an answer.

Сделай радио потише.
ZdYEHlahy rAHdyeeo pahtEEshih.

Lower the radio.

Выключи телевизор.
VUIklyoochee tihlihvEEzahr.

Turn off the television set.

Тебе нельзя смотреть эту программу!
TihbYEH nihl'zYAH smahtrYEHt'
EHtoo prahgrAHmmoo!

You may not watch that program!

Приготовь уроки!
PreegahtAWv' oorAWrkee!

Do your lessons!

Выключи телевизор, когда ты
готовишь уроки.
VUIklyoochee tihlihvEEzahr, kahgdAH
tui gahtAWveesh oorAWrkee.

No TV when you are doing lessons.

Ты сделал/-а домашнюю работу? (m/f)
Tui zdYEHlahl/-ah dahmAHshnyooyoo
rahbAWtoo?

Did you do your home work?

Перестань говорить по телефону!
PihrihstAHn' gahvahrEEt' pah tihlihfAWnoo!

Stop talking on the phone!

О чём ты говоришь?
Ah chyawm tui gahvahrEEsh?

What are you talking about?

/Я говорю/ Ты говоришь/ сам/-а с собой?
/Yah gahvahrYOO/ Tui gahvahrEEsh/
sahm/-AH sahbOY? (m/f)

/Am I/ Are you/ talking to/ myself/ yourself/?

Перестань играть на компьютере!
PihrihstAHn' eegrAHt'nah
kahmp'YOOtihryih!

Stop playing on the computer!

Уже поздно приглашать твоих друзей.
OozhYEH pAWznah preeglahshAHt'
tvahEEkh droozYEHy.

It's too late to invite friends.

Книгу пора вернуть (в библиотеку).
KnEEgoo pahrAH vihrnOOt' (fbeebleeahtYEHkoo).

Your book is due
(at the library).

Тебе нужно вернуть книгу в библиотеку.
TihbYEH nOOzhnah vihrnOOt'
knEEgoo fbeebleeahtYEHkoo.

You have to return the book to the library.

Тебе нужно идти на занятия по музыке.
TihbYEH nOOzhnah eetEE nah zahn-
YAHteeyih pah mOOzuikyih.

You have to go to your music lessons.

Пристегни ремень безопасности.
PreestihgnEE rihmYEHn' bezahpAHs-
nahstee.

Fasten your seat belt.

Из-за кого у нас так вырос счёт за
телефон?
Eez-zah kahvAW oo nahs tahk vUIrahs
shchyawt zah tihlihfAWn?

Who's been running up the phone bill?

Ты/ должен/ должна/ покормить собаку.
Tui / dAWlzhihn/ dahlzhnAH/ pahkahr-
mEET' sahbAHkoo. (m/f)

You should feed the dog.
(now)

Сейчас твоя очередь...
SihchAHs tvahYAH AWchihriht'...

It's your turn ...

выгуливать собаку,
vuigOOleevaht' sahbAHkoo,

to walk the dog,

выносить мусор.
vuinahsEEt' mOOsahr.

to carry out the garbage.

Сними наушники!
SneemEE nahOOshneekee!

Take off the head set!

Приходи домой вовремя!
PreekhahdEE dahmOY vAWvrihmyih!

Come home on time!

Когда ты придёшь домой с игровой
площадки?
KahgdAH tui preedYAWsh dahmOY
seegrahvOY plahschAHdkee?

When will you come home
from the playground?

Не опаздывай! Ты опоздал/-а! (m/f)
Nih ahpAHzduivahy! Tui ahpahzdAHl/-ah!

Don't be late! You're late!

Я боюсь, что уже слишком поздно.
Yah bahYOOs', shtaw oozhYEH
slEEshkahm pAWznah.

I'm afraid it's already too
late.

Откуда ты идёшь?
AhtkOOdah tui eedYAWsh?

Where are you coming
from?

Я иду из своей комнаты.
Yah eedOO eez svahYEHy kAWmnahtui.

I'm coming from my
room.

Я вернусь домой вовремя.
Yah vihrnOOs' dahmOY vAWvrihmyih.

I'll be home on time.

Я всегда прихожу домой/ рано/ вовремя/.
Yah fsyegdAH preekhahzhOO/ dahmOY/
rAHnah/ vAWvrihmyih/.

I always come home/
early/ on time/.

Я не знаю, когда я приду домой.
Yah nih znAHyoo, kahgdAH yah preedOO dahmOY.

I don't know when I'll be
home.

Я не хочу слушать жалобы!
Yah nih khahchOO slOOshaht'
zhAHlahbui!

I don't want to hear any
complaints!

Об этом не может быть и речи!
Ahb EHtahm nih mAWzhiht buit'ee
rYEHchee!

That's out of the question!

No sooner said than done.

Сказано – сделано

Помощь по дому

Helping at Home

Your children are happiest when they are imitating adults in their lives. This includes the work they do. You and your children working together are a natural setting for speaking Russian together.

Помочь тебе (+ inf.)......?
PahmAWch' tihbYEH.......?

Could I help you ......?

Помоги мне (+ inf.)...
PahmahgEE mnYEH:

Help me:

 накрыть на стол,
 nahkrUIt' nah stawl,

 set the table,

 пододвинуть этот стул (ближе к столу).
 pahdahdvEEnoot' EHtaht stool
 (blEEzhih kstahlOO).

 move the chair (nearer
 the table).

Ты можешь положить салфетки (на стол).
Tui mAWzhish pahlahzhEEt' sahlfYEtkee.

You can put the napkins on
(the table).

Накрой на стол, пожалуйста.
NahkrOY nah stawl, pahzhAHloostah.

Set the table, please.

Убери со стола, пожалуйста.
OobihrEE sah stahlAH, pahzhAHloostah.

Clear the table, please.

Помоги мне/ помыть/ вытереть/ посуду.
PahmahgEE mnYEH/ pahmUIt'/ vUItih-riht'/ pahsOOdoo.

Help me/ wash/ dry/ the dishes.

Помоги мне постирать бельё.
PahmahgEE mnYEH pahsteerAHt' bihlYAW.

Help me do the laundry.

В раковине полно грязной посуды.
VrAHkahveenyih pahlnAW grYAHz-noy pahsOOdui.

The sink is filled with dirty dishes.

Помоги мне/ убрать в доме/ убраться/.
PahmahgEE mnYEH/ oobrAHt' fdAWmyih/ oobrAHt'sah/.

Help me/ clean up around the house/ clean up/.

Убирай всё!
OobeerAHy fsyaw!

Clean up everything!

Помоги мне постелить постель.
PahmahgEE mnYEH pahstihlEEt' pahstYEHl'.

Help me make the bed.

Помоги мне стирать.
PahmahgEE mnYEH steerAHt'.

Help me do the washing. (laundry)

Ты постелил/-а кровать? (m/f)
Tui pahstihlEEl/-ah krahvAHt'?

Did you make your bed?

Почему нет?
PahchihmOO nyeht?

Why not?

Ты заставляешь меня много работать!
Tui zahstahvlAHihsh mnYAH mnAWgah rahbAWtaht'!

You make me work a lot!

Мама подметает пол.
MAHmah pahdmihtAHiht pawl.

Mommy's sweeping the floor.

Папа пылесосит коврик.
PAHpah puilihsAWseet kAWvreek.

Daddy is vacuuming the rug.

Пылесос работает очень шумно.
PuilihsAWs rahbAWtahiht AWchihn' shOOmnah.

The vacuum cleaner is noisy.

Какая пыль! Давай вытирать (пыль)!
KahkAHyah puil'! DahVAHy vuiteerAHt'!

What dust! Let's dust!

Держи тряпку в руке и три.
DihrzhEE trYAHpkoo vrookYEH ee tree.

Hold the dust cloth in your hand, and rub.

Так, хорошо.
Tahk, khahrahshAW.

That's right.

Я шью юбку для тебя.
Yah shyoo YOOpkoo dlyah tihbYAH.

I'm sewing a skirt for you.

Помоги папе приготовить обед.
PahmahgEE pAHpyih preegahtAWveet' ahbYEHT.

Help Daddy make lunch.

Мама печёт торт.
MAHmah pihchYAWt tawrt.

Mommy's baking a cake.

Хочешь помочь мне печь печенье?
KhAWchihsh pahmAWch' mnYEH pyehch' pihchYEHn'yih?

Do you want to help me bake cookies?

Насыпь муку.
NahsUIp' mookOO.

Pour in the flour.

Я взбиваю яйца.
Yah vzbeevAHyoo YAHytsah.

I'm beating the eggs.

Мы смешиваем сахар и масло.
Mui smYEHsheevahihm sAHkhahr ee mAHslah.

We mix the sugar and butter.

Нам нужен разрыхлитель?
Nahm nOOzhihn rahzruihkhlEEtihl'?

Do we need baking
powder?

Меси тесто как следует.
MyehsEE tYEHstah kahk slYEHdooiht.

Knead the dough
thoroughly.

Мы печём его в духовке.
Mui pihchYAWm yihvAW
fdookhAWfkyih.

We bake them in the oven.
(cookies)

Поставь часы на полчаса.
PahstAHf' chahsUI nah pahlchahsAH.

Set the clock for half an
hour.

Печенье готово.
PihchEHn'yih gahtAWvah.

The cookies are done.

Ты не можешь мне помогать гладить.
Tui nih mAWzhihsh mnYEH pahmahgAHt' glAHdeet'.

You cannot help me iron.

Ты можешь мне помочь сортировать и
складывать одежду.
Tui mAWzhihsh mnYEH pahMAWCH'
sahrteerahvAHt' ee sklAHduivaht'
ahdYEHzhdoo.

You can help me sort and
fold the clothes.

После уборки мы можем почитать
рассказ.
PAWslih oobAWrkee mui mAWzhihm
pahcheetAHt' rahskAHs.

After cleaning, we can
read a story.

Ты готов/-а читать со мной? (m/f)
Tui gahtAWf/ gahtAWvah/ cheetAHt'
sah mnoy?

Are you ready to read
with me?

Перед тем как идти играть, тебе нужно
убрать комнату.
PYEHrihd tyehm kahk eetEE eegrAHt',
tihbYEH nOOzhnah oobrAHt' kAWmnahtoo.

Before playing, you must
clean your room.

Убири кастрюли в шкаф.
OobeerEE kahstrYOOlee fshkahf.

Put the pots back in the cabinet.

Ты хотел/-а бы пойти (со мной) по магазинам?   (m/f)
Tui khahtYEHLl/ah bui pahytEE (sah mnoy) pah mahgahzEEnahm?

Would you like to go shopping (with me)?

Я хочу купить что-нибудь поесть.
Yah khahchOO koopEEt' shtAW-neeboot' pahYEHst '.

I want to buy something to eat.

Можно я пойду с тобой ?
MAWzhnah yah pahydOO stahbOY?

May I come with you?

Ты можешь идти.
Tui mAWzhish eetEE.

You may be excused.

Что ты хочешь купить?
Shtaw tui khAWchish koopEEt'?

What do you want to buy?

Мне нужно много разных вещей.
MnYEH nOOzhnah mnAWgah rAHz-nuikh vihschYEHy.

I need all kinds of things.

Вот тебе на твои расходы.
Vawt tihbYEH nah tvahEE rahskhAWdui.

Here is your allowance.

Тебе нужно купить новую одежду.
TihbYEH nOOzhnah koopEEt' nAWvooyoo ahdYEHzhdoo.

You need to buy new clothes.

Можешь помочь мне завернуть подарок?
MAWzhihsh pahmAWch' mnYEH zahvihrnOOt' pahdAHrahk?

Can you help me wrap the present?

Нам нужно сгрести снег.
Nahm nOOzhnah sgrihstEE snyehk.

We have to shovel the snow.

Помоги мне косить лужайку.
PahmahgEE mnYEH kahsEEt ' loozhAHykoo.

Help me mow the lawn.

Сажай семена рядами.
SahzhAHy sihmihnAH ryihdAHmee.

Plant the seeds in a row.

Здесь так много сорняков.
Zdyehs' tahk mnAWgah sahrnyihkAWf.

There are so many weeds.

Нам нужно прополоть сад...
Nahm nOOzhnah prahpahlAWt' saht...

We have to weed the
garden...

...чтобы растения могли расти.
...shtAWbui rahstYEHneeyih mahglEE
rahstEE.

...so the plants will grow.

Ты будешь помогать мне поливать
огород?
Tui bOOdihsh pahmahgAHt' mnYEH
pahleevAHt' ahgahrAWt?

Will you help me water the
vegetable garden?

Не копай слишком/ много/ глубоко/.
Nih kahpAHy slEEshkahm /mnAWgah/
gloobahkAW/.

Don't dig too/ wide/
deeply/.

Копай здесь на клумбе.
KahpAHy zdyehs' nah klOOmbyih.

Dig here in the flowerbed.

Осторожно, смотри: гусеницы!
AhstahrAWzhnah, smahtrEE:
gOOsihneetsui!

Watch out for the caterpillars!

Помоги мне сгрести листья.
PahmahgEE mnYEH sgrihstEE lEEst'yih.

Help me rake the leaves.

Брось листья в бак для мусора.
Braws' lEEst'yih fbahk dlyah mOOsahrah.

Throw the leaves in the
garbage can.

Положи разбрызгиватель здесь.
PahlahzhEE rahsbrUIsgeevahtihl'zdyehs'.

Put the sprinkler here.

Ты не можешь помогать мне обрезать
деревья.
Tui nih mAWzhihsh pahmahgAHt'
mnYEH ahbrihzAHt' dihrYEHv'yih.

You cannot help me prune
the trees.

Это слишком опасно.
EHTah slEEshkahm ahpAHsnah.

It's too dangerous.

Мы будем строить вагон.
Mui bOOdihm stROYeet'vahgAWn.

We'll build a wagon.

Можешь ли ты очистить этот кусок
дерева?
MAWzhihsh lee tui ahchEEsteet' EHtaht koosAWk dYEHrihvah?

Can you sand this piece
of wood?

Распили эту доску пополам.
RahspeelEE EHtoo dAWskoo pahpah-
lAHm.

Saw this board in two.

Вбей гвоздь.
Fbyehy gvawst'.

Hammer the nail.

Ты хочешь посмотреть?
Tui khawchihsh pahsmahtrYEHt'?

Do you want to watch?

Помоги мне чинить машину.
PahmahgEE mnYEH cheenEEt'
mahshEEnoo.

Help me work on the car.

/Помой/ Пропылесоси/ машину.
/PahmOY/ PrahpuilihsAWsee/
mahshEEnoo.

/Wash/ Vacuum/ the car.

Подмети тротуар.
PahdmihtEE trahtooAHr.

Sweep the sidewalk.

Помоги мне подключить компьютер.
PahmahgEE mnYEH pahdklyoochEET'
kahmp'YOOtihr.

Help me hook up the
computer.

Положи мои вещи на место.
PahlahzhEE mahEE vYEHschee nah
mYEHstah.

Put my things back.

Like teacher, like pupil.

Каков поп, таков и приход

Уроки в доме   School at Home

A popular trend is taking place in America where children and parents are taking charge of their own education. They are doing this at home. Children having classes at home instead of in a school building will find these phrases useful. Of course, these sentences will apply to a classroom situation as well.

Школьный автобус только что проехал!   The school bus just went by!
ShkAWl'nuiy ahftAWboos tAWl'kah
shtaw prahYEHkhahl!

Нам пора начинать работать.   Time for us to start work.
Nahm pahrAH nahcheenAHt'
rahbAWtaht'.

Что мы будем делать сегодня?   What will we do today?
Shtaw mui bOOdihm dYEHlaht' sih-
vAWd nyih?

Давайте (pl) будем точны.   Let's be punctual.
DahvAHytyih bOOdihm tAWchnui.

70

На чём мы (вчера) остановились?
Nah chyawm mui (fchihrAH) ahstahnah-
vEElees'?

Where did we stop
(yesterday)?

Какой сегодня день?
KahkOY sihvAWdnyih dyehn'?

What day is today?

Какой день будет завтра?
KahkOY dyehn' bOOdiht zAHvtrah?

What day is tomorrow?

Когда мы начнём нашу работу?
KahgdAH mui nachnYAWm nAHshoo
rahbAWtoo?

When will we begin our
work?

Давайте (pl) продолжать работать.
DahvAHytyih prahdahlzhAHt'
rahbAWtaht'.

Let's go on working.

Я/ рад/ рада/, что нам не нужно
сегодня идти в школу. (m/f)
Yah/ raht/ rAHdah/, shtaw nahm nih
nOOzhnah sihvAWdnyih eetEE
fshkAWloo.

I'm glad we don't have to
go to school today.

Что ты изучаешь?
Shtaw tui eezoochAHihsh?

What are you studying?

Я (сейчас) изучаю русский язык.
Yah (sihchAHs) eezoohAHyoo
rOOskee yihzUIk.

I'm studying Russian
(now).

Говори по-русски.
GahvahrEE pah-rOOskee.

Speak Russian.

Повторяй за мной.
PahftahrYAHy zah mnoy.

Repeat after me.

Зачем надо изучать русский язык?
ZahchYEHm nAHdah eezoochAHt'
rOOskee yihzUIk?

Why must we study
Russian?

Я/ рад/ рада/, что мы сегодня дома. (m/f)
Yah/ raht/ rAHdah/, shtaw mui sihvAWdnyih dAWmah.

I'm glad we're home
today.

Этот проект о рыбах,
EHtaht prahYEHkt ah ruibAHkh,

This fish project,

проект о картах ,
prahYEHkt ah kAHrtakh,

map project,

проект о животных,
prahYEHkt ah zheevAWtnuikh,

animal project,

трудный/ труден. (long/ short form)
TrOOdnuiy/ trOOdihn.

is difficult.

Время терпит.
VrYEHmyih tYEHrpeet.

There's plenty of time.

Нам нужно:
Nahm nOOzhnah:

We need:

скотч, степлер,
skawtch, stYEHplihr,

scotch tape, a stapler,

ножницы, плакатный картон.
nAWzhneetsui, plahkAHtnuiy
kahrtAWn.

scissors, poster board.

Скобок нет.
SkAWbahk nyeht.

There are no staples.

Как долго ты занимаешься
математикой?
Kahk dAWlgah tui zahneemAHihshsah
mahtihmAHteekoy?

How long have you been
working on math?

Нам нужно изучать естественные науки?
Nahm nOOzhnah eezoochAHt' ihs-
tYEHstvihnuiyih nahOOkee?

Do we have to study
science?

В котором часу мы начинаем уроки?
FkahtAWrahm chahsOO mui nah-
cheenAHihm oorAWkee?

At what time are we start-
ing lessons?

Мы будем заниматься/ утром/ днём/.
Mui bOOdihm zahneemAHt'sah/
OOtrahm/ dnyawm/.

We'll study/ in the
morning/ in the evening/.

Разве у тебя нет хорошей книги?
RAHZvyih oo tihbYAH nyeht khah-
rAWshyehy knEEgee?

Don't you have a good
book?

Тебе хочется почитать?
TihbYEH khAWchihtsah pahcheetAHt'?

Do you feel like reading?

Мне сейчас нечего читать.
MnYEH sihchAHs nYEHchihvah
cheetAHt'.

I have nothing to read.

Мне сейчас не хочется это делать.
MnYEH sihchAHs nih khAWchihtsah
EHtah dYEHlaht'.

I don't feel like doing it
now.

Не ленись.
Nih lihnEEs'.

Don't be lazy.

Скажи мне, если ты меня не поймёшь.
SkahzhEE mnYEH, YEHslee tui mnYAH
nih pahymYAWsh.

Tell me if you don't
understand me.

Ты/ должен (m)/должна (f)/ это знать.
Tui/ dAWLzhihn/ dahlzhnAH/ EHtah znaht'.

You should know this.

Тебе это понятно?
TihbYEH EHtah pahnYAHtnah?

Does this make sense?

Можно задать тебе вопрос?
MAWzhnah zahdAHt' tihbYEH vahprAWs?

Can I ask you a question?

Помоги сестре в математике.
PahmahgEE sihstrYEH fmahtihmAHt eekyih.

Help your sister with math.

Покажи сестре...
PahkahzhEE sihstrYEH...

...как ей делать математику.
...kahk yehy dYEHlaht' mahtihmAHt-
eekoo.

Математика для меня труднее,
а история легче.
MahtihmAHteekah dlyah mnYAH
troodnYEHih, ah eestAWreeyih
lYEHchyeh.

Сложи эти цифры.
SlahzhEE EHtee tsEEfrui.

Ты хочешь задать вопрос?
Tui khAWchihsh zahdAHt'
vahprAWs?

Мама, у меня застрял дырокол.
MAHmah, oo mnYAH zahstrYAHl
duirahkAWl.

Что тебе нужно?
Shtaw tihbYEH nOOzhnah?

Тебе нужен карандаш? (m)
TihbYEH nOOzhihn kahrahndAHsh?

Тебе нужна книга? (f)
TihbYEH nOOzhnah knEEgah?

Тебе нужно зеркало? (n)
TihbYEH nOOzhnah zYEHrkahlah?

Что мне делать? Мне скучно.
Shtaw mnYEH dYEHlaht'?
MnYEH skOOshnah.

Show your sister...

...how to do her math.

Math is harder for me,
but history is easier.

Add these figures.

Do you want to ask a
question?

Mom, the hole punch is
stuck.

What do you need?

Do you need a pencil?

Do you need a book?

Do you need a mirror?

What is there for me to do?
I'm bored.

Давайте (pl) сделаем небольшой перерыв.
DahvAHytyih zdYEHlahihm nihbahl'-
shOY pihrihrUIf.

Let's take a little break.

Мы будем работать в саду.
Mui bOOdihm rahbAWtaht' fsahdOO.

We'll work in the garden.

Когда мы вернёмся, мы
KahgdAH mui vihrnYAWmsah, mui

When we come back,
we'll:

будем читать,
bOOdihm cheetAHt',

read,

подключимся к интернету,
pahdklYOOcheemsah kihntihrnYEHtoo,

go on-line,

пошлём кате электронную почту,
pahshlAWm kAHtyih ehlihktrAWn-
ooyoo pAWchtoo,

E-mail Katya,

испечём печенье для дяди Петра,
eespihchAWm pihchEHn'yih dlyah
dYAHdee pihtrAH,

bake cookies for Uncle
Peter,

будем рисовать рисунок.
bOOdihm reesahvAHt' reesOOnahk.

paint a picture.

Какого цвета цветы?
KahkAWvah tsvYEHtah tsvYEHtui?

What color are the flowers?

Нам нужно учиться.
Nahm nOOzhnah oochEEt'sah.

We have to study.

Нам нужно писать
Nahm nOOzhnah peesAHt'

Do we have to have
(to write)

контрольную по истории,
kahntrAWl'nooyoo pah eestAWree-ee,

a history quiz,

контрольную по географии?
kahntrAWl'nooyoo pah gihahgrAHfee-ee?

a geography quiz?

Я люблю учиться.
Yah lyooblYOO oochEEt'sah.

I like to study.

Учи уроки.
OochEE oorAWkee.

Study your lessons.

Давай (s) начинать урок.
DahvAHy nahcheenAHt' oorAWk.

Let's begin our lesson.

Занимайся своими уроками!
ZahneemAHysah svahEEmee
oorAWkahmee!

Get busy with your lessons!

Лучше я следующим делом
приготовлю урок. (по истории)
LOOchih yah slYEHdooyooscheem
dYEHlahm preegahtAWvlyoo
oorAWk. (pah eestAWree-ee)

I'd better do my (history)
lesson next.

У тебя довольно времени это сделать.
Oo tihbYAH dahvAWl'nah vrYEHmihnee EHtah zdYEHlaht'.

You have enough time to
do that.

Ты/ должен/ должна/ выучить это. (m/f)
Tui /dAWLzhihn/ dahlzhnAH/
vUIoocheet' EHtah.

You've got to learn that.

Постарайся сделать лучше.
PahstahrAHysah zdYEHlaht' lOOchih.

Try to do better.

Я помогу тебе как можно больше.
Yah pahmahgOO tihbYEH kahk
mAWzh nah bAWl'shih.

I will help you as much
as possible.

Мне нужно дополнительное время
для музыки.
MnYEH nOOzhnah dahpahlnEEtihl'-
nahyih vrYEHmyih dlyah mOOzuikee.

I need extra time for my
music.

Можно я пропущу урок истории?
MAWzhnah yah prahpooschOO
oorAWk eestAWree-ee?

May I skip history?

Мои цветные карандаши пропали.
MahEE tsvyehtnUIyih kahrahndahshEE
prahpAHlee.

My crayons are missing.

Ты их потерял/-а?   (m/f)
Tui eekh pahtihrYAHl/-ah?

Have you lost them?

Кто-нибудь их видел?
Ktaw-neebOOt' eehk vEEdihl?

Has anyone seen them?

Ты много работал/-а.   (m/f)
Tui mnAWgah rahbAWtahl/-ah.

You have worked a lot.

Ты заслуживаешь что-нибудь приятное!
Tui zahslOOzheevahihsh shtaw-neebOOt'
preeYAHtnahyih!

You deserve something
nice!

Мне/ легко/ трудно/ (делать/ самому (m)
/самой (f)/).
MnYEH/ lihkAW/ trOOdnah/(dYEHlaht'/
sahmAWmoo/ sahmOY/).

This is/ easy/ difficult/
for me (to do myself).

Как продвигается твоя работа?
Kahk prahdveegAHihtsah tvahYAH
rahbAWtah?

How is your work coming
along?

Ты выучил/-а свой урок?   (m/f)
Tui vUIoocheel/-ah svoy oorAWk?

Do you know your lesson?

Я выучил/-а свой урок.(m/f) Я учу урок.
Yah vUIoocheel/-ah svoy oorAWk.
Yah oochOO oorAWk.

I know my lesson. I'm
doing my lesson.

Я не выучил/-а своего урока.   (m/f)
Yah nih vUIoocheel/-ah svahyihvAW
oorAWkah.

I don't know my lesson.

Выброси ненужную бумагу в корзину.
VUIbrahsee nihnOOzhnooyoo boomAH-
goo fkahrzEEnoo.

Throw the waste paper
in the basket.

77

The end crowns the work.

Конец — Делу венец

Похвала

Praise

All the ways to say, "You're tops!" "None better!" "Wonderful, wonderful you!"
and many, many more. Use this chapter *often*. You and your child will *LOVE* it.

Для меня ты лучше всех!
Dlyah mnYAH tui lOOchih fsyekh!

You're my number one!

Какой красивый голос!
KahkOY krahsEEvuiy gAWlahs!

What a beautiful voice!

Ты хорошо/ ходишь/ чертишь/ поёшь/.
Tui khahrahshAW/ khAWdeesh/
chYEHrteesh/ pahYAWsh/.

You/ walk/ draw/ sing/ well.

Как хорошо ты/ кушешь/ пишешь/
плаваешь/ играешь/!
Kak khahrahshAW tui/ kOOshihsh/ pEE-
shish/ plAHvahihsh/ eegrAHihsh/!

How well you/ eat/ write/
swim/ play/!

Ты удивительный/-ая! (m/f)
Tui oodeevEEtihl'nuiy/-ahyih!

You're wonderful!

Как ты/ мил/ мила/! (m/f)
Kahk tui/ meel/ meelAH /!

How (sweet) cute you are!

/Какой/-ая ты сильный/-ая! (m/f)
/KahkOY/ KahkAHyih tui/ sEEl'nuiy/
sEEl'nahyah!

How strong you are!

Какой/-ая смелый/-ая! (m/f)
/KahkOY/ KahkAHyih/ smYEHl'
uiy/-ahyah!

How brave you are!

Это платье тебе идёт.
EHtah plAHt'yih tihbYEH eedYAWt.

This dress suits you.

Какие у теья красивые глаза!
KahkEEyih oo tihbYAH krahsEEVuiyih
glahzAH!

What pretty eyes you have!

Я люблю/ твои глазки/ ручки/ пузик/.
Yah lyooblYOO/ tvahEE glAHSkee/
rOOchkee/ pOOzeek/.

I love/ your eyes/ hands/
your tummy/.

Ты выглядишь, как/ принцесса/ принц/.
Tui vUIglyihdeesh, kahk/ preentsYEHsah/
preents/.

You look like a /princess/
prince/.

Ты хорошая девочка!
Tih khahrAWshahyih dYEHvahchkah!

You are a good girl!

Ты хороший мальчик!
Tih khahrAWsheey mAHL'cheek!

You are a good boy!

Ты/ добрый/ добрая/ . (m/f)
Tui / dAWbruiy/ dAWbrahyah/.

You are generous.

Будь всегда милым!
Boot' fsegdAH mEEluim!

Always be nice!

Ты мне нравишся.
Tui minYEH nrAHveeshsah.

I like you.

Я тебя люблю.
Yah tihbYAH lyooblYOO.

I love you.

Браво! Бис! (Theatre)
BrAHvah! Bees!

Bravo! Encore!

Хорошо сделано! Ещё!
KhahrahshAW zdYEHlahnah!
YihschYAW!

Well done! Again!

Мне нравится, что ты играешь тихо один.
MnYEH nrAHveetsah, shtaw tui
eegrAHihsh tEEkhah ahdEEn.

I like the way you play
quietly by yourself.

Папытайся ещё раз!
PahpuitAHysah yihschYAW rahs!

Try again!

Не сдавайся!
Nih zdahvAHysah!

Don't give up!

Какая замечательная идея!
KahkAHyah zahmihchAHtihl'nahyih eedYEHyah!

What a great idea!

Ты становишься лучше и лучше!
Tui stahnAWveeshsah lOOchih ee
lOOchih!

You're getting better and
better!

Я/ благодарен/ благодарна/ тебе за
твою помощь. (m/f)
Yah/ blahgahdAHrihn/ blahgahdAHrnah
/ tihbYEH zah tvahYOO pAWmahsch.

I am thankful for your help.

Ты был/-а терпелив/-а когда я говорил/-а
по телефону. (m/f)
Tui buil/-AH tihrpihlEEf/ tihrpihlEEvah/
kahgdAH yah gahvahrEEl/-ah pah
tihlihfAWnoo.

You were patient while I
was on the telephone.

Это очень мило с твоей стороны.
EHtah AWchihn' mEElah stvahYEHy
stahrahnUI.

That's kind of you.

Ты/ добрый / добрая/! (m/f)
Tui/ dAWbrui/ dAWbrahyih/!

You are kind!

Ты уже убрал /-а в своей комнате. (m/f)
Tui oozhYEH oobrAHl/-ah fsvah-
YEHy kAWmnahtyih.

You cleaned your room.

У тебя золотые руки.
Oo tihbYAH zahlahtUIyih rOOkee.

You are good with your hands.

Ты можешь гордиться собой!
Tui mAWzhihsh gahrdEEt'sah
sahbOY!

You can be proud of yourself!

All that glitters is not gold.

Не всё зо́лото, что блести́т

Поку́пки   ## Shopping

This area of foreign language conversation may be unpredictable. When children are young, they enjoy speaking Russian. As they grow more sensitive, they may not wish to seem different by speaking a foreign language others might overhear. Assure them that you understand their feelings. Resume speaking Russian outside the store or in the car. You might want to "play store" at home using Russian.

Мне ну́жно соста́вить спи́сок. MnYEH nOOzhnah sahstAHveet' spEEsahk.	I have to make a list.
Мне на́до сходи́ть за хле́бом, молоко́м, мя́сом. MnYEH nAHdah s-khahdEEt' zah khlYEHbahm, mahlahkAWm, mYAHsahm.	I need to buy bread, milk, meat.
Я е́ду в магази́н за хле́бом. Yah YEHdoo fmahgahzEEn zah khlYEHbahm.	I'm driving to the store to get bread.

Я собираюсь поехать:
Yah sahbeerAHyoos' pahYEHkhaht':

    на склад лесоматериалов,
    nah sklaht lihsohmahtihreeAHlahf,

    в питомник,
    fpeetAWmneek,

    на заправочную станцию,
    nah zahprAHvahchnooyoo stAHntseeyoo,

    в магазин игрушек,
    fmahgahzEEn eegrOOshihk,

    в парикмахерскую,
    fpahreekmAHkherskooyoo,

    в булочную,
    fbOOlahshnooyoo,

    в гастроном,
    fgahstrahnAWm,

    в прачечную,
    fprAHchihshnooyoo,

    в спортивный магазин,
    fspahrtEEvnuiy mahgahzEEn,

    в магазин деликатесов,
    fmahgahzEEn dihleekahtYEHsahf,

    в универмаг,
    booneevihrmAHk,

    в аптеку,
    fahptYEHkoo,

    в мясной магазин,
    fmyihsnOY mahgahzEEn,

I intend to go: (by car)

to the lumber yard,

to the nursery,

to the gas station,

to the toy store,

to the barber shop,

to the bakery,

to the grocery store,

to the laundromat,

to the sports store,

to the delicatessen,

to the department
store,

to the drugstore,

to the butcher shop,

в рыбный магазин,
frUIbnuiy mahgahzEEn,

to the fish store,

в банк,
fbahnk,

to the bank,

в книжный магазин,
fknEEzhnuiy mahgahzEEn,

to the book store,

в обувной магазин,
vahboovnOY mahgahzEEn,

to the shoe store,

в музыкальный магазин,
fmoozuikAHl'nuiy mahgahzEEn,

to the music store,

в торговый центр,
ftahrgAWvuiy tsEHntr,

to the mall,

на почту,
nah pAWchtoo,

to the post office,

в видео магазин.
vEEdihoh mahgahzEEn.

to the video store.

Я еду в супермаркет.
Yah YEHdoo fsoopihrmAHrkiht.

I am going (by vehicle)
to the supermarket.

Здесь распродажа. Мне нужно купить...
Zdyehs' rahsprahdAHzhah. MnYEH
nOOzhnah koopEEt'...

There's a sale, here.
I have to buy...

Где можно купить...?
Gdyeh mAWzhnah koopEEt'...?

Where can I buy...?

Мне нужно вернуть...
MnYEH nOOzhnah vihrnOOt'...

I must return...
(bring something back)

Что ты купишь в этом магазине?
Shtaw tui kOOpeesh vYEHtahm
mahgahzEEnyih?

What will you buy in this
store?

Что ты купишь на свой доллар? Shtaw tui kOOpeesh nah svoy dAWlahr?	What will you buy with your dollar?
Давай(те) поедим на/ лифте/ эскалаторе/. DahvAHy(tyih) pahYEHdihm nah/ lEEftyih/ eskahlAHtahryih/.	Let's take the/ elevator/ escalator/.
/Сиди/ Оставайся/ в тележке для покупок. /SeedEE/ AhstahvAHysah/ ftihlYEHzh- kyih dlyah pahkOOpahk.	/Sit/ stay/ in the shopping cart.
Просунь ногу через отверстие. PrahsOOn' nAWgoo chYEHrihs ahtvYEHrsteeyih.	Put your foot through the opening.
Вы не могли бы помочь, пожалуйста? Vui nih mahglEE bui pahmAWch', pahzhAHloostah? (polite)	Can you help me?
Что-нибудь ещё? Shtaw-neebOOt'yihschYAW?	Anything else?
Нам нужно купить новую одежду. Nahm nOOzhnah koopEEt' nAWvoo- yoo ahdYEHzhdoo.	We need to buy new clothes.
Я хочу купить: Yah khahchOO koopEEt':	I want to buy:
что-нибудь/ хорошее/ симпатичное/, shtAW-neeboot'/ khahrAWshihyih/ seempahtEEchnahyih/,	something/ nice/ pleasant,
что-нибудь новое, shtAW-neeboot' nAWvahyih,	something new,
что-то белое. shtAW-tah bYEHlahyih.	something white.
Мне хотелось бы... MnYEH khahtYEHlahs' bui...	I'd like...

Нам нельзя истратить все свои деньги.
Nahm nihl'zYAH eestrAHteet' fsyeh
svahEE dYEHn'gee.

We cannot spend all our
money.

Мы не можем это купить.
Mui nih mAWzhihm EHtah koopEEt'.

We cannot buy that.

Я осталась (почти) без денег.
Yah ahstAHlahs' (pahchtEE) byehs
dYEHnihk.

I'm (almost) out of
money.

Сколько у тебя при себе денег?
SkAWl'kah oo tihbYAH pree sihbYEH
dYEHnihk?

How much money do you
have? (on you)

Это слишком много денег.
EHtah slEEshkahm mnAWgah.
dYEHnihk.

That's too much money.
(to be carrying)

У меня нет денег.
Oo mnYAH nyeht dYEHnihk.

I have no money.

У меня/ немного/ много/ денег.
Oo mnYAH/ nihmnAWgah/ mnAWgah/
dYEHnihk.

I have/ a little/ a lot of/
money.

Копи свои деньги.
KahpEE svahEE dYEHn'gee.

Save your money.

Это слишком дорого.
EHtah slEEshkahm dAWrahgah.

That's too expensive.

Может быть, что-нибудь подешевле.
MAWzhiht buit', shtAW-neeboot'
pahdihshYEHvlyih.

Perhaps something
cheaper.

Это/ удачная/ неудачная/ покупка.
Ehtah/ oodAHchnahyih/
nihoodAHchnahyih/ pahkOOpkah.

That's a/ good/ bad/ buy.

Мне нужно денег.
MnYEH nOOzhnah dYEHnihk.

I need some money.

/Продавец/ Продавщица/ там.
/PrahdahvYEHts/ PrahdahvschEEtsah/
tahm.

The /salesman/ sales-woman/ is over there.

Сколько это стоит?
SkAWl'kah EHtah stAWiht?

How much is it?

Сколько с меня?
SkAWl'kah smnYAH?

How much do I owe you?

Нам нужно это купить?
Nahm nOOzhnah EHtah koopEEt'?

Should we buy it?

Стоит ли нам это покупать?
StAWiht lee nahm EHtah pahkoopAHt'?

Should we buy it?
(Not likely)

Давай купим/ его(m/n)/ её(f)/ для мамы.
DahvAHy kOOpeem/ yihvAW/ yihYAW/
dlyah mAHmui.

Let's buy it for mother.

Не покупай это.
Nih pahkoopAHy EHtah.

Don't buy that.

Я покупаю/ его (m/n)/ её (f)/ их (pl)/.
Yah pahkoopAHyoo/ yihvAW/ yihYAW/
eekh/.

I'm buying/ it/ them/.

Какого размера это пальто?
KahkAWvah rahzmYEHrah EHtah
pahl'tAW?

What size is this coat/?

Какой это размер?
KahkOY EHtah rahzmYEHr?

What size is it?

Дай мне посмотреть.
Dahy mnYEH pahsmahstrYEHt'.

Let me see that.

Примерь.
PreemYEHr'.

Try it on.

Какой/ Какая/ тебе больше нравится? /KahkOY/ KahkAHyih/ tihbYEH bAWl'shih nrAHveetsah? (m/f)	Which do you prefer?
/Этот/ Эта/ Это/ слишком/ — (m/f/n) /EHtaht/ EHtah/ EHtah/ slEEshkahm/	This is too —
— узок/ узка/ узко/. — OOzahk/ ooskAH/ ooskAW/.	– tight.
— просторен / просторна / просторно/. — prah stAWrihn/ prahstAWrnah/ prahstAWrnah/.	– loose.
Это пальто тебе/ велико/ мало/. (n) EHtah pahl'tAW tihbYEH/ vihleekAW/ mahlAW/.	This coat is/ large/ small/ for you.
Эта шляпа тебе/ велика/ мала/. (f) EHtah shlYAHpah tihbYEH/ vihleekAH/ mahlAH/.	This hat is/ large/ small/ for you.
Этот свитер тебе/ велик/ мал/. (m) EHtaht svEEtihr tihbYEH/ vihlEEK/ mahl/.	This sweater is/ large/ small/ for you.
/Он /Она /Оно/ на тебе превосходно сидит. /Awn/ AhnAH/ AhnAW/ nah tihbYEH prih-vahskhAWdnah seedEEt. (m/f/n/)	It fits (you) perfectly.
Тебе очень идёт. TihbYEH AWchihn' eedYAWt.	It looks good on you.
Посчитай сдачу. PahscheetAHy zdAHchoo.	Count your change.
Где мы с тобой встретимся? Gdyeh mui stahbOY fstrYEHteemsah?	Where shall we meet?
Встречаемся здесь через час. FstrihchAHihmsah zdyehs' chYEHrihs chahs.	Meet me here in an hour.

Будь рядом/ со мной/ с мамой/ с папой/.
Boot' rYAHdahm/ sah mnoy/ smAHmoy/
spAHpoy/.

Stay near/ me/ Mom/ Dad/.

Как ты думаешь, папе понравится?
Kahk tui dOOmahihsh, pAHpeh
pahnrAHveetsah?

Do you think Dad would
like it?

У вас есть хозяйственная сумка?
Oo vahs yehst' khahzYAHystvihnahyih
sOOmkah?

Do you have a shopping
bag?

Магазин полон народу.
MahgahzEEn pAWlahn nahrAWdoo.

The store is crowded.

Не иди у меня за спиной.
Nih eedEE oo mnYAH zah speenOY.

Don't walk behind me.

Где касса?
Gdyeh kAHssah?

Where is the cashier?

Следующий!
SlYEHdooscheey!

Next!

Мы можем просто побродить по
магазинам.
Mui mAWzhihm prAWstah pahbrah-
dEEt' pah mahgahzEEnahm.

We can go window
shopping.

/Выход / Вход/ там.
/VUIkhawt/ Fkhawt/ tahm.

/The exit/ entrance/ is
over there.

Мы ищем/ игрушки/ мебель /одежду/.
Mui EEschihm/ eegrOOshkee/
mYEHbihl'/ ahdYEHzhdoo/.

We're looking for / toys/
furniture/ clothing/.

Стоянка запрещена!
StahYAHnkah zahprihschenAH!

No parking!

one for all and all for one.

Один за всех, все за одного

Весело!   Fun !

If this chapter's pages don't have paint stains, water marks, and gum sticking the pages together, you are not getting all there is to wring out of these pages! Be sure to add some of your sentences that are appropriate. I have found it helpful to place sentences and phrases on 3 x 5 cards wherever I need them until the phrase is part of my thinking.

Можно мне пойти на улицу?	Can I go outside?
MAWzhnah mnYEH pahytEE nah OO-leetsoo?	
Можешь/ тебе разрешается/:	You/ can/ are allowed to/ may/:
MAWzhihsh/ tihbYEH rahzrihshAHihtsah/:	
поиграть во дворе,	play in the yard,
paheegrAHt' vah dvahrYEH,	
пойти на детскую площадку,	go to the playground,
pahytEE nah dYEHtskooyoo plah-schAHtkoo,	

пойти на (футбольное, бейсбольное) поле, pahytEE nah (footbAWl'nahyih, byehys-bAWl' nahyih) pAWlyih,	go to the (soccer, base-ball) field ,
сходить/ к своему другу/ к своей подруге/. skhahdEEt'/ ksvahyihmOO drOOgoo/ ksvahYEHy pahdrOOgyih/. (m/f)	go to your friend's house.

Спроси их, хотят ли они поиграть: SprahsEE eekh, khahtYAHt lee ahnEE paheegrAHt':	Ask them if they want to play:
во врача и медсестру, vah vryahchAH ee mehdsihstrOO,	doctor and nurse,
в магазин, fmahgahzEEn,	shopkeeper,
на компьютере, nah kahmp'YOOtihryih,	computer,
в прятки. fprYAHtkee.	hide and seek.

Можно/ с тобой (s)/ с вами(pl)/ поиграть? MAWzhnah/ stahbOY (s)/ svAHmee (pl)/ paheegrAHt'?	May I play with you?
Можно мне тоже прийти? MAWzhnah mnYEH tAWzhih preetEE?	May I come, too?
Я/ больше/ выше/ тебя. Yah/ bAWl'shih/ vUIshih/ tihbYAH.	I'm/ bigger/ taller/ than you.
Я сильнее тебя. Yah seel'nYEHyih tihbYAH.	I'm stronger than you.
Я старше тебя. Yah stAHrshih tihbYAH.	I'm older than you.

Моя собака лучше твоей.
MahYAH sahbAHkah lOOchih
tvahYEHy.

My dog is nicer than yours.

Мой велосипед лучше твоего.
Moy vihlahseepYEHt lOOchih
tvahyihvAW.

My bike is better than yours.

Моя комната лучше твоей.
MahYAH kAWmnahtah lOOchih
tvahYEHy.

My room is better than yours.

САМОЛЁТЫ — AIRPLANES

Пилот диспетчеру.
PeelAWt deespYEHtchihroo.

Pilot to tower.

Пожалуйста, пристегните ремни
безопасности.
PahzhAHloostah, preestehgnEEtyih
rihmnEE behzahpAHsnahstee.

Please fasten your seat belt.

Вылетаю!
VuilihtAHyoo!

I'm taking off!

Сбавить газ!
SbAHveet' gahs!

Throttle down!

Я иду на посадку!
Yah eedOO nah pahsAHdkoo!

I'm landing!

У нас заканчивается топливо!
Oo nahs zahkAHncheevahihtsah
tAWpleevah!

We're running out of fuel!

Очистить взлётную полосу!
AhchEEsteet' vzlYAWtnooyoo pahlahsOO!

Clear the runway!

Сколько времени лететь до Москвы?
SkAWl'kah vrYEHmihnee lihtYEHt'
dah mahskVUI?

How long is the flight to Moscow?

92

ВО ДВОРЕ/ В САДУ — IN THE YARD/ GARDEN

Иди и играй/ на улице/ дома/.
EedEE ee eegrAHy/ nah OOleetsih/
dAWmah/.

Go/ outside/ inside /
and play.

Играй/ во дворе /в песочнице/.
EegrAHy/ vah dvahrYEH/ fpehsAWch-
neetsih/.

Play in the/ yard/ sand-
box/.

Ты хочешь пускать мыльные пузыри?
Tui khAWchish pooskAHt' mUIl'-
nuiyih poozuirEE?

Do you want to blow
bubbles?

Не играй в грязи!
Nih eegrAHy fgryahzEE!

Don't play in the dirt.

Не рви цветы, пожалуйста!
Nih rvEE tsvyehtUl, pahzhAHloostah!

Please don't pick the
flowers!

Можешь плавать в бассейне, если я
с тобой.
MAWzhihsh plAHvaht' fbahssYEHnyih,
YEHslee yah stahbOY.

You can swim in the pool
if I am with you.

Прыгни с вышки, как я тебе показывал/-а.
PrUIgnee svUIshkee, kahk yah tihbYEH
pahkAHzhuivahl/-ah. (m/f)

Jump off the diving board
as I've shown you.

Будь/ осторожен/ осторожна/, когда ты
взбираешь на дерево.   (m/f)
Boot'/ ahstahrAWzhihn/ ahstahrAWzh-
nah/, kahgdAH tui vzbeerAHihsh nah
dYEHrihvah.

Be careful when you are
climbing the tree.

Вы оба можете сидеть в вагоне.
Vui AWbah mAWzhihtyih seedYEHt'
fvahgAWnyih.

You both can sit in the
wagon.

Здесь достаточно места для двоих.
Zdyehs' dahstAHtahchnah mYEHstah
dlyah dvahEEkh.

There's enough room for
two.

_____

Не уходи со двора.   Don't leave the yard.
Nih ookhahdEE sah dvahrAH.

БЕЙСБОЛ — BASEBALL

(Note: The game of baseball does not exist in Russia. It is included
here for its American fans.)

Твоя очередь (бить битой).   It's your turn (at bat).
TvahYAH AWchihriht (beet' bEEtoy).

Лови! Бросай!   Catch! Throw!
LahvEE! BrahsAHy!

Держи биту за собой.   Hold the bat behind you
DihrzhEE bEEtoo zah sahbOY.

Следи за мячом.   Keep your eye on the ball.
SlyehdEE zah myahchAWm.

Ударяй (битой).   Swing (with the bat).
OodahrYAHy (bEEtoy).

Не попал/-а по мячу. (m/f) Мимо!   You missed the ball.
Nih pahpAHl/-ah pah myahchOO.   Missed!
MEEmah!

Ты выиграл/-а пробег! (m/f)   You scored a run!
Tui vUIeegrahl/-ah prahbYEHk!

Это был хороший бросок!   That was a good throw!
EHtah buil khahrAWsheey brahsAWk!

ЕЗДА НА ВЕЛОСИПЕДЕ — BICYCLING

Поставь ноги на педали.   Put your feet on the pedals.
PahstAHf nAWgee nah pihdAHlee.

Не крути так быстро педали.   Don't pedal so fast.
Nih krootEE tahk bUIstrah pihdAHlee.

У тебя/ держу/ придерживаю/.
Oo tihbYAH/ dihrzhOO/ pree-
dYEHrzheevahyoo/.

I've got a hold of you.
(firmly/ lightly)

Старайся поддерживать равновесие.
StahrAHysah pahdYEHrzheevaht'
rahvnahvYEHseeyih.

Try to keep your balance.

Дай я попробую!
Dahy yah pahprAWbooyoo!

Let me try!

Держись за руль!
DihrzhEEs' zah rool'!

Hold on to the handlebars!

Поезжай прямо.
PahyehzhAHY prYAHmah.

Go straight.

Поезжай/ направо/ налево/.
PahyehzhAHY/ nahprAHvah/ nah-
lYEHvah/.

Go/ right/ left/.

Крути педали!
KrootEE pihdAHlee!

Keep pedaling!

Ты очень хорошо едешь на велосипеде.
Tui AWchihn' khahrahshAW YEHdihsh
nah vihlahseepYEHdyih.

You're riding your bicycle
very well.

Не езди на велосипеде по улице!
Nee YEHzdee nah vihlahseepYEHdyih
pah OOleetsih!

Don't ride your bicycle
in the street!

Там слишком сильное движение.
Tahm slEEshkahm sEEl'nahyih dvee-
zhYEHneeyih.

There's too much traffic.

Ты едешь слишком быстро!
Tui YEHdihsh slEEshkahm bUIstrah!

You're going too fast!

Нажми на тормоз!
NahzhmEE nah tAWrmahs!

Put on the brake!

95

Не свались с велосипеда.
Nih svahlEEs' svihlahseepYEHdah.

Don't fall off your bicycle.

Ты/ свалился/ свалилась/ с велосипеда.
Tui/ svahlEElsah/ svahlEElahs'/ svihlahseepYEHdah. (m/f)

You fell off your bicycle.

Тебе нужно надеть шлем.
TihbYEH nOOzhnah nahdYEHt'
shlyehm.

You need to put on your
helmet.

НАСТОЛЬНЫЕ ИГРЫ — BOARD GAMES

Ты хочешь поиграть/ в шашки/
в шахматы / в настольную игру/?
Tui khAWchihsh paheegrAHt'/
fshAHshkee/ fshAHkhmahtui/ fnah-
stAWl' nooyoo eegrOO/?

Do you want to play/
checkers/ chess/ a board
game/?

Чья очередь?
Ch'yah AWchihriht'?

Whose turn is it?

Опять моя (твоя) очередь.
AhpYAHt' mahYAH (tvahYAH)
AWchihriht'.

It's my (your) turn again.

Я брошу кубики.
Yah brAWshoo kOObeekee.

I'll throw the dice.

Я хочу синюю фигуру.
Yah khahchOO sEEnyooyoo feegOOroo.

I want the blue figure.
(piece)

Твоя фигура не на том месте.
TvahYAH feegOOrah nih nah tawm
mYEHstyih.

Your piece is in the wrong
place.

Ты не так идёшь.
Tui nih tahk eedYAWsh.

You're going the wrong
way.

Пойди/ вперёд/ назад/.
PahydEE /fpihrYAWt/ nahzAHt/.

Move/ forward/ backward/.

Ты не честно играешь.
Tui nih chYEHstnah eegrAHihsh.

You aren't playing fairly.

Ты/ должен/ должна/ мне заплатить.
Tui/ dAWlzhihn/ dahlzhnAH/ mnYEH
zahplahtEEt'. (m/f)

You have to pay me.

Ты мне/ должен/ должна/. (m/f)
Tui mnYEH/ dAWlzhihn/ dahlzhnAH/.

You owe me money.

Я заплачу.
Yah zahplahchOO.

I'll pay.

Ты/ выиграл/-a/ проиграл/-a. (m/f)
Tui/ vUIeegrahl/-ah/ praheegrAHl/-ah.

You have/ won/ lost/.

ЛОДКИ — BOATS

Корабль отправляется!
KahrAHbl' ahtprahvlYAHihtsah!

All aboard!

Мы уезжаем из порта.
Mui ooYEHzzhahihm eez pAWrtah.

We're leaving port.

Мы идём в плавание в Россию.
Mui eedYAWm fplAHvahneeyih.
vrahsEEyoo.

We're sailing to Russia.

Лодка тонет!
LAWdkah tAWniht!

The boat is sinking!

Человек за бортом!
ChihlahvYEHk zah bahrtAWm!

Man overboard!

Покиньте корабль!
PahKEEN'tyih kahRAHbl'!

Abandon ship!

Спускайте спасательную шлюпку!
SpooskAHytyih spahsAHtihl'nooyoo
ShlYOOpkoo!

Lower the life boats!

Мы едем кататься на лодке.
Mui YEHdihm kahtAHt'sah nah
lAWdkyih.

We're going boating.

Помедленнее!
PahmYEHdlihnihyih!

Slow down!

Я буду управлять лодкой.
Yah bOOdoo ooprahvlYAHt' lAWdkoy.

I'll drive the boat.

Ты можешь кататься на водных лыжах.
Tui mAWzhihsh kahtAHt'sah nah
vAWdnuikh lUIzhahkh.

You can water-ski.

Выйди и оттолкни!
VUIdee ee ahtahlknEE!

Get out and push off!

Сходи за вёслами!
SkhahdEE zah vYAWslahmee!

Get the oars!

Я погребу. (or) Я буду грести.
Yah pahgryehbOO. Yah bOOdoo gryehstEE.

I'll row.

Греби как можно быстрее.
GryehbEE kahk mAWzhnah buistrYEHyih.

Row as fast as you can.

ПОХОД — CAMPING

Сколько времени мы хотим стоять
лагерем?
SkAWl'kah vrYEHmihnee mui khah-
tEEm stahYAHt' lAHgihrihm?

How long do we want to
camp?

Нам нужна новая палатка.
Nahm noozhnAH nAWvahyah
pahlAHtkah.

We need a new tent.

Я/ рад/ рала/,что у нас есть наш фургон.
Yah/ raht/ rAHdah/, shtaw oo nahs
yehst' nahsh foorgrAWn.   (m/f)

I am happy that we have
our camper.

Давайте (pl) поставим палатку. DahvAHytyih pahstAHveem pah-lAHtkoo.	Let's pitch the tent
Я хочу, чтобы лагерь стоял прямо на озере. Yah khahchOO, shtAWbui lAHgihr' stahYAHl prYAHmah nah AWzehryih.	I want a camp site right on the lake.
Положи свой спальный мешок в палатку. PahlahzhEE svoy spAHL'nuiy mihsh-AWk fpahlAHtkoo.	Put your sleeping bag inside the tent.
Установи плитку. OostahnahvEE plEEtkoo.	Set up the stove.
Это идеальное место для лагеря. EHtah eedihAHl'nahyih mYEHStah dlyah lAHgihryih.	This is a perfect place to camp.

МАШИНЫ — CARS

Машина сломалась. MahshEEnah slahmAHlahs'.	The car broke down.
Она дальше не едет. AhnAH dAHl'shih nih YEHdiht.	It doesn't go any more.
Почему машина не едет? PahchihmOO mahshEEnah nih YEHdiht?	Why doesn't the car go?
Подтолкни машину. Я поведу. PahtahlknEE mahshEEnoo. Yah pahvihdOO.	Push the car. I'll drive.
Проверьте (pl.), пожалуйста, масло, воду, аккумулятор. PrahvYEHr'tyih, pahzhAHloostah, mAHslah, vAWdoo, ahkoomoolYAHtahr.	Check the oil, the water, the battery, please.
Заправьте (pl.) машину! ZahprAHv'tyih mahshEEnoo!	Fill 'er up!

Заведи машину в гараж.
ZahvihdEE mahshEEnoo fgahrAHsh.

Drive the car into the garage.

Дай задний ход.
Dahy zAHdneey khawt.

Back up.

Быстро! Дай газу!
BUIstrah! Dahy gAHzoo!

Step on it! Give it the gas!

Посигналь! Нажми на сигнал!
Pahseegnahl'! NahzhmEE nah seegnAHl!

Honk! Blow the horn!

Мой любимый автомобиль.........
Moy lyoobEEmuiy ahftahmahbEEl'.........

My favorite car is........

РАСКРАСЬ И ПРИКЛЕЙ — COLOR and PASTE

Ей можно взять цветные карандаши.
Yey mAWzhnah vzyaht' tsvyehtnUIyih kahrahndahshEE.

She may use the crayons.

Раскрась солнце жёлтым цветом.
RahskrAHs' sAWntsih zhYAWltuim tsvYEHtahm.

Color the sun yellow.

Нарисуй птицу каким хочешь цветом.
NahreesOOy ptEEtsoo kahkEEm khAWchish tsvYEHtahm.

Paint the bird the color you like.

Вырежи эту картинку из журнала.
VUIrihzhee EHtoo kahrtEEnkoo eez zhoornAHlah.

Cut this picture out of the magazine.

Приклей картинку на бумагу (клейкой лентой).
PreeklYEHy kahrtEEnkoo nah boomAHgoo (klYEHykoy lYEHntoy).

Tape the picture on the paper (with sticky tape).

Приклей это осторожно на бумагу.
PreeklYEHy EHtah ahstahrAWzhnah nah boomAHgoo.

Paste this carefully on the paper.

Сложи лист бумаги.
SlahzhEE leest boomAHgee.

Fold the paper.

Не порви бумагу.
Nih pahrvEE boomAHgoo.

Don't tear the paper. (Be careful.)

Собери клочки бумаги.
SahbihrEE klahchkEE boomAHgee.

Pick up the scraps of paper.

Нарисуй:
NahreesOO:

Draw:

  круг,
  krook,

the circle,

  треугольник,
  trihoogAWl'neek,

the triangle,

  прямоугольник,
  pryahmahoogAWl'neek,

the rectangle,

  и квадрат (вот так).
  ee kvahdrAHt (vawt tahk).

and the square (like this).

/Раскатай/ Разомни/ глину.
/RahskahtAHy/ RahzahmnEE/ glEEnoo.

/Roll/ Knead/ the clay.

КОМПЬЮТЕР — COMPUTER

Ты хочешь поиграть в компьютерную игру?
Tui khAWchihsh paheegrAHt' fkahmp'-YOOtihrnooyoo eegrOO?

Do you want to play a computer game?

Мы это распечатаем.
Mui EHtah rahspihchAHtahihm.

We'll print it out.

Это неправильное сообщение.
EHtah nihPRAHVeel'nahyih sahahb-schEHneeyih.

There's an error message.

Мы можем осуществить поиск, на компьютере.
Mui mAWzhihm ahsooschyehstvEEt' pAWeesk, nah kahmp'YOOtihryih.

We can make a computer search.

КУКЛЫ — DOLLS

Как зовут твою куклу?
Kahk zahVOOT tvahYOO kOOkloo?

What is your doll's name?

Твоя кукла красивая?
TvahYAH kOOklah krahsEEvahyih?

Is your doll pretty?

Покорми свою куклу.
PahkahrmEE svahYOO kOOkloo.

Feed your doll.

Одень куклу.
AhdYEHn' kOOkloo.

Dress the doll.

Мне нужно её причесать.
MnYEH nOOzhnah yihYAW preechih-sAHt'.

I have to comb her hair.

Положи её аккуратно.
PahlahzhEE yihYAW ahkoorAHtnah.

Put her down gently.

Не шлёпай куклу так сильно!
Nih shlYAWpahy kOOkloo tahk sEEl'nah!

Don't spank the doll so hard!

Ты можешь сделать модель платья на компьютере.
Tui mAWzhihsh zdYEHlaht' mah-dYEHl' plAH'tyih nah kahmp'YOOtihryih.

You can design a dress on the computer.

УГАДАЙ — GUESS WHAT !

(Bold faced vowels indicate stressed syllable.)

Мне нравятся красные плащи. Я
большой. Я нападаю с помощью рогов.
Какое я животное?   (бык)

I like red capes. I'm large.
I charge with my horns.
What animal am I? (bull)

Я сижу на кувшинках. Я говорю:
"Ква-ква!"
Я ловлю насекомых языком.
Какое я животное?   (лягушка)

I sit on water-lilies. I say,
"Croak!Croak!" I catch
insects with my tongue.
Which animal am? (frog)

Я лаю, рычу и гоняю кошек.
Я говорю: "Гав-гав!"
Какое я животное?   (собака)

I bark, growl and chase
cats. I say, "Bow-wow"!
Which animal am I? (dog)

Я ношу детёнышей в сумке.
У меня четыре лапы; но
я не умею бегать. Я прыгаю.
Какое я животное?   (кенгуру)

I carry my young in my
pouch. I have four legs;
I cannot run. I hop.Which
animal am I? (kangaroo)

Я хожу величественно и кукарекаю.
У меня есть перья.
Я говорю: "Кукареку!"
Какое я животное?   (петух)

I strut and crow. I have
feathers. I say, "Cock-a-
doodle-doo!" Which
animal am I? (rooster)

ДЕТСКАЯ ПЛОЩАДКА — PLAYGROUND

Иди и прячься!
EedEE ee prYAHch'sah!

Go and hide!

Смывайся! Сматывайся!
SmuivAHysah! SmAHtuivahysah!

Scram!

Где ты? Где я?
Gdyeh tui? Gdyeh yah?

Where are you?
Where am I?

Я здесь! (or) Вот и я!
Yah zdychs'! (or) Vawt ee yah!

Here I am!

Давай качаться на качелях!
DahvAHy kahchAHt'sah nah kah-
chYEHlyikh!

Let's swing on the swing!

Не прыгай с качелей!
Nih prUIgahy skahchYEHlyehy!

Don't jump off the swing!

Не стой (ногами) на качелях!
Nih stoy (nahgAHmee) nah kah-
chYEHlyikh!

Don't stand on the swing!

Не качайся на качелях стоя на ногах.
Nih kahchAHysah nah kahchYEHlyihkh
stAWyih nah nahgAHkh.

Don't swing while stand-
ing.

Я тебя слегка раскачиваю.
Yah tihbYAH slihKAH rahskAHch-
eevahyoo.

I am pushing you gently.

Не закрывай глаза!
Nih zahkruivAHy glahzAH!

Don't close your eyes!

Держись за/ поручни горки/ каруселей/.
DihrzhEEs zah/ pAWroochnee
gAWrkee/ kahroosYEHlyehy/.

Hold on to the /slide/
merry-go-round/.

Спускайся с горки!
SpooskAHysah sgAWrkee!

Slide down the slide!

Воздушный змей падает.
VahsdOOshnuiy smyehy pAHdahiht.

The kite is falling.

Недостаточно сильный ветер.
NihdahstAHtahchnah sEEl'nuiy
vYEHtihr.

There's not enough
wind.

Держи верёвку крепко!
DihrzhEE vihrYAWvkoo krYEHpkah!

Hold the tail tightly!

Хочешь скакалку?
KhAWchihsh skahkAHlkoo?

Do you want to jump
rope?

Стреляй стеклянными шариками
в круг.
StrihlYAHy stihklYAHnuimee
shAHreekahmee fkrook.

Shoot (like a gun) the
marbles into the circle.

Надуй воздушный шарик.
NahdOOy vahsdOOshnuiy shAHreek.

Blow up the balloon.

Шарик сдувается!
ShAHreek sdoovAHihtsah!

Air is leaking from the
balloon!

Помоги! Пожар! Включи сирену!
PahmahgEE! PahzhAHr! FklyoochEE
seerEHnoo!

Help! Fire! Sound the
siren!

Позвони в пожарное отделение!
PahzvahnEE fpahzhAHrnahyih
ahtdyihlYEHneeyih!

Call the fire department!

Следуй за лидером!
SlYEHdooy zah lEEdihrahm!

Follow the leader!

Встаньте (pl.) в круг.
VstAHn'tyih fkrook.

Stand in a circle.

Коньки затупились.
Kahn'kEE zahtoopEElees'.

My skates are dull.

Их нужно поточить.
Eehk nOOzhnah pahtahchEEt'.

They need to be sharp-
ened

Держись за меня. Я тебе помогу.
DihrzhEEs' zah mnYAH. Yah tihb-
YEH pahmahgOO.

Hold on to me. I'll help
you.

Отталкивайся с левой ногой.
AhtAHlkeevahysah slYEHvoy
nahgOY.

Push off with your left
foot.

Подними правую ногу.
PahdneemEE prAHvooyoo nAWgoo.

Lift the right foot.

Прокатись на коньках вокруг катка. Skate around the rink.
PrakahtEEs' nah kahn'kAHkh vahkrOOk
kahtkAH.

Ты готов/-а кататься на коньках спиной. You're ready to skate
Tui gahtAWf/ gahtAWvah kahtAHt'- backwards.
sah nah kahn'kAHkh spEEnoy. (m/f)

ФУТБОЛ — SOCCER

Веди мяч! Dribble the ball!
VihdEE myahch!

Не трогай мяч руками. Don't touch the ball with
Nih trAWgahy myahch rookAHmee. your hands.

Ударь мяч в ворота! Kick the ball into the
OodAHr' myahch vvahrAWtah! goal!

/Следуй / Беги/ за мячом! /Go/ Run/ after the ball!
/SlYEHdooy/ BihgEE/ zah
myahchAWMm!

Забей гол! Score a goal!
ZahbYEHy gawl!

Ты забил/-а гол! Гол! (m/f) You have scored a goal!
Tui zahbEEl/-ah gawl! Gawl! Goal!

Мо-лод-цы! Мо-лод-цы! Way to go!
Mah-lahd-tsUI! Mah-lahd-tsUI!

Гола нет! No goal!
GAWlah nyeht!

Мяч был в воротах! The ball was in the goal!
Myahch buil vvahrAWtahk!

Передай (мне) мяч! Pass the ball (to me)!
PihrihdAHy (mnYEH) myahch!

Мы проиграли!
Mui praheegrAHlee!

We've lost!

В офсайде!
VawfsAHydyih!

Off sides!

СПОКОЙНЫЕ ИГРЫ — QUIET GAMES

Поиграй в спокойную игру и отдохни.
PaheegrAHy fspahkOYnooyoo
eegrOO ee ahtdahkhnEE.

Play a quiet game and rest.

Давай соберём пазл (вместе).
DahvAHy sahbihrYAWm pawzl
(vmYEHstyih).

Let's do a puzzle (together).

Давай положим этот кусок здесь.
DahvAHy pahlAWzheem EHtaht
koosAWk zdyehs'.

Let's put this (puzzle) piece in there.

Ты думаешь, этот кусок сюда подходит?
Tui dOOmahihsh, EHtaht koosAWk
syoodAH pahdkhAWdeet?

Do you think this piece goes here?

Этот кусок не подходит.
EHtaht koosAWk nih pahdkhAWdeet.

This piece doesn't fit.

Какого куска не хватает?
KahkAWvah kooskAH nih khvahtAHiht?

Which piece is missing?

Этот пазл слишком/ лёгкий/ трудный/!
EHtaht pawzl slEEshkahm/ lYAWkeey/
trOOdnuiy/!

This puzzle is too/ easy/ hard/!

Смотри в окно!
SmahtrEE vahknAW!

Look out the window!

Что ты видишь...
Shtaw tui vEEdeesh...

What do you see...

за деревом,
zah dYEHrihvahm,

behind the tree,

за мной,
zah mnoy,

behind me,

за матерью,
zah mAHtihr'yoo,

behind mommy,

под столом?
pawt stahlAWm?

under the table?

Я ничего не вижу.
Yah neechihvAW nih vEEzhyoo.

I don't see anything.

Давай сыграем в карты.
DahvAHy suigrAHihm fkAHrtui.

Let's play a game of cards.

Ты можешь разобрать свою коллекцию марок.
Tui mAWzhihsh rahzahbrAHt' svahYOO kahLYEHktseeyoo mAHrahk.

You can sort your stamp collection.

ПОЕЗДА И ГРУЗОВИКИ — TRAINS and TRUCKS

Поезд отправляется!
PAWihst ahtprahvlYAHihtsah!

All aboard!

Билеты, пожалуйста!
BeelYEHtui, pahzhAHloostah!

Tickets, please!

Сколько стоит проезд?
SkAWl'kah stAWeet prahYEHst?

What does the fare cost?

Я еду задним ходом.
Yah YEHdoo zAHdneem khAWdahm.

I'm driving backwards.

Я нагружаю свой грузовик.
Yah nahgroozhAHyoo svoy groozahvEEk.

I'm loading my truck.

Ты доставляешь нефть в нефтевозе?
Tui dahstahvlYAHihsh nyehft' vnihftih-
vAWzyih?

Are you delivering oil
 in your oil truck?

Это не нефтевоз; это грузовик для
перевозки скота.
EHtah nih neftihvAWs; EHtah
groozahvEEk dlyah pihrihvAWskee
skahtAH.

This is not an oil truck;
it's a cattle truck.

Мне нравится джип.
MinYEH nrAHveetsah zheep.

I like the (4 x 4) pick-up.

Когда я получу водительские права,
я хочу...
KahgdAH yah pahloochOO vahdEEtihl'-
skeeyih prahvAH, yah khahchOO...

When I have my license,
I want...

Веселись!
VihsihlEEs'!

Have fun! Enjoy yourself!

The more the merrier!

Чем больше, тем лучше

В субботу днём   Saturday Afternoon

The opportunities for using Russian on Saturdays are unlimited. Saturdays were made for Russian! Chores to do using Russian, visits to friends using Russian, shopping, outings, sports. The list is endless as you can see.

Давайте/ сходим/ пойдём/ в кино/ в торговый центр/. DahvAHytyih/ skhAWdeem /pahy-dyAWm/fkeenAW/ ftahrgAWvuiy tsYEHntr/.	Let's go to the/ movies/ mall/.
Могли бы ....и ....пойти с нами? MahglEE bui....ee....pahytEE snAHmee?	May ....and ....come with us?
Что мы будем делать? Shtaw mui bOOdihm dYEHlaht'?	What shall we do?
Давай(те)(pl) отправляться. DahvAHy(tyih) ahtprahvlYAHt'sah	Let's get going. (Let's start.)

Я бы лучше/ пошёл/ пошла/ на детскую площадку. (m/f)
Yah bui lOOchih/ pahshYAWl/ pah-shlAH/ nah dYEHtskooyoo plah-schAHdkoo.

I'd rather go to the play-ground.

Это (гораздо) веселее.
EHtah (gahrAHzdah) vihsihlEHyih.

It's (much) more fun.

Ну, пойдём(те)! (pl)
Noo, pahdYAWMm(tyih)!

Let's go! (on foot)

Ну, поедем(те)! (pl)
Noo, pahYEHdihm(tyih)!

Let's go! (by vehicle)

Останься дома.
AhstAHn'sah dAW-mah.

Stay home.

Ты уже закончил/-а работу по дому?
Tui oozhYEH zahkAWncheel/-ah rahbAWtoo pah dAWmoo? (m/f)

Have you finished your chores?

После работы по дому ты можешь/ идти на улицу/ идти играть/.
PAWSlih rahbAWtui pah dAWmoo tui mAWzhihsh/ eetEE nah OOleetsoo/ eetEE eegrAHt'/.

After chores you can /go out/ go play/.

Ты без дела (or) Тебе нечего делать?
Tui byehs dYEHlah? (or) TihbYEH nYEHchihvah dYEHlaht'?

Have you nothing to do?

Сейчас мне нечего делать.
SihchAHs mnYEH nYEHchihvah dYEHlaht'.

I have nothing to do now.

Куда мне идти?
KoodAH mnYEH eetEE?

Where am I to go?

Мне некуда идти.
MnYEH nYEHkoodah eetEE.

I have no where to go.

111

Мне не с кем говорить.
MnYEH nYEH skyehm gahvahrEEt'.

I have no one to talk with.

Есть школьная пьеса.
Yehst' shkAWl'nahyah p'YEHsah.

There is a school play.

Есть кукольный спектакль в библиотеке.
Yehst' kOOkahl'nuiy spihktAHkl' fbeeb-
leeahtYEHkyih.

There's a puppet show at
the library.

Есть выставка:
Yehst' vUIstahvkah:

There is an exhibit:

поездов,
pahyehzdAWf,

train show,

садовых принадлежностей,
sahdAWvuikh preenahdlYEHzhnahstehy,

garden show,

автомашин.
ahftahmahshEEn.

car show.

Мы поедем на/ метро/ автобусе/.
Mui pahYEHdihm nah/ mihtrAW/
ahftAWboosyih/.

We'll take the /subway/ bus/.

Нам можно поесть в ресторане?
Nahm mAWzhnah pahYEHst'
vrehstahrAHnyih?

Can we eat out?
(asking permission)

Мне хочется есть в ресторане.
MnYEH khAWchihtsah yehst' frehstahrAHnyih.

I want to eat in a restaurant.

Тебе нужно пойти к зубному врачу.
TihbYEH nOOzhnah pahytEE kzoob-
nAWmoo vrahchOO.

You have to go to the dentist.

Хочешь, не хочешь, а идти надо.
KhAWchish, nih khAWchish, ah
eetEE nAHdah.

You have to go whether you
want to or not.

112

Нужно подогнать твои пластинки.
NOOzhnah pahdahgnAHt' tvahEE
plahstEEnkee.

Your braces need to be
adjusted.

Нет, тебе нельзя покрасить волосы
в зелёный цвет!
Nyeht, tihbYEH nihlz'YAH pahkrAH-
seet' vAWlahsui fzihlYAWnuiy tsvyeht!

No, you cannot dye your
hair green!

Сядь в машину!
Syaht' vmahshEEnoo !

Get in the car!

Мы поедем прокатиться на машине.
Mui pahYEHdihm prahkahtEEt'sah
nah mahshEEnyih.

We'll go for a ride.

Позвони...........и мы/ пойдём/ поедем/:
PahzvahnEE......ee mui/ pahydYAWm/
pahYEHdihm/:

Call up ......and we'll go
(foot/ vehicle):

кататься на роликовых досках,
kahtAHt'sah nah rAWleekahvuikh
dAWskahk,

skateboarding,

кататься на роликах,
kahtAHt'sah nah rAWleekakh,

roller skating,

кататься на роликовых коньках.
kahtAHt'sah nah rAWleekahvuikh
kahn'kAHk.

roller blading.

Давай послушаем мой новый
компакт- диск.
DahvAHy pahslOOshahihm moy
nAWvuiy kahmpAHkt-deesk.

Let's listen to my new CD!

Я бы лучше/ пошёл/ поехал/ на рыбалку.
Yah bui lOOchih/ pahshYAWl/
pahYEHkhahl/ nah ruibAHlkoo. (m/f)

I would rather go fishing.

У нас есть наживка и крючки.
Oo nahs yehst' nahzhEEvkah ee kryoochkEE.

We have the bait and hooks.

113

Ты забыл/-а удочку. (m/f)
Tui zahbUIl/-ah OOdawchkoo.

You forgot the fishing rod.

Ты хочешь пойти на рыбалку?
Tui khAWchish pahytEE nah
ruibAHlkoo?

Would you like to go
fishing?

Я поймал/-а рыбу! (m/f)
Yah pahymAHl/-ah rUIboo!

I caught a fish!

Не могли бы мы закончить постройку
дома на дереве?
Nih mahglEE bui mui zahkAWncheet'
pahstrOYkoo dAWmah nah dYEHrih-
vyih?

Can't we finish building
the tree house?

Я принесу молоток, гвозди, пилу и доски.
Yah preenihsOO mahlahtAWk, gvAWs-
dee, peelOO ee dAWskee.

I'll get the hammer, nails,
saw and boards.

Давай (те) (s/pl) встретимся во дворе.
DahvAHy (tyih) vstrYEHteemsah vah
dvahrYEH.

Let's meet in the back yard.

Пойдём на чердак!
PahydYAWm nah chihrdAHk!

Let's go to the attic!

Давай/ смотреть/ посмотрим/ футбол
(по телевизору).
DahvAHy/ smahtrYEHt'/ pahsmAW-
treem/ footbAWl (pah tihlihvEEzahroo).

Let's watch soccer (on TV).

Давай (s) читать комиксы.
DahvAHy cheetAHt' kAWmeeksui.

Let's read comic-books.

Пойдём/ на пляж/ на озеро/.
PahydYAWm/ nah plyahzh/ nah AWzihrah/.

Let's go to the/ beach/ lake/.

Пойдём/ на море/ в бассейн/.
PahydYAWm/ nah mAWryih/
fbahsYEHn/.

Let's go to the/ ocean/
pool/.

Идём плавать.
EedYAWm plAHvaht'.

Let's go swimming.

Идём кататься на водных лыжах.
EedYAWm kahtAHt'sah nah
vAWdnuikh lUIzhahkh.

Let's go waterskiing.

Я принесу полотенца,
Yah preenihsOO pahlahtYEHntsah,

I'll bring the towels,

пляжный зонтик и стул,
plYAHzhnuiy zAWnteek ee stool,

the beach umbrella/
chair,

ведро и лопату.
vihdrAW ee lahpAHtoo.

the pail and shovel.

Вот мы и здесь!
Vawt mui ee zdyehs'!

Here we are!

Небо ясное.
NYEHbah YAHsnahyih.

The sky is clear.

Расстели подстилку/ на солнце/ в тени/.
RahstyehlEE pahtstEElkoo/ nah sAWntsih ftihnEE/.

Spread the blanket in the/
sun/ shade/.

Море/ бурное/ спокойное/.
MAWryih/ bOOrnahyih/ spahkOY-
nahyih/.

The sea is/ rough/ calm/.

Плавай здесь. Здесь мелко.
PlAHvahy zdyehs'. Zdyehs' mYEHlkah.

Swim here. It is shallow
here.

Мы можем/ делиться друг с другом/
по очереди пользоваться/ надувным
матрасом.
Mui mAWzhihm/ dyehlEEt'sah drook
sdrOOgahm/ pah AWchihrihdee
pAWl'zahvaht'sah/ nahdoovnUIm/
mahtrAHsahm.

We can/ share/ take turns
using/ the air mattress.

/ Выходи/ Выйди/ из воды.
/VuikhahdEE/ vUIydee/ ees vahdUI.

Come out of the water.

Тебе нельзя идти обратно в воду.
TihbYEH nihl'zYAH eetEE ah-brAHtnah vvAWdoo.

You are not allowed back in the water.

Ты только что поел/-a! (m/f)
Tui tAWl'kah shtaw pahYEHl/-ah!

You have just eaten!

Тебе слишком холодно.
TihbYEH slEEshkahm khAWlahdnah.

You're too cold.

Ты дрожишь от холода.
Tui drahzhEEsh awt khAWlahdah.

You're shivering with cold.

Не простудись.
Nih prahstoodEEs'.

Don't catch cold.

Здесь есть медузы!
Zdyehs' yehst' mihdOOzui!

There are jelly fish here!

Ну, уже поздно.
Noo, oozhYEH pAWznah.

It's getting late.

Почему бы нам не:
PahchihmOO bui nahm nih:

Why don't we:

поискать ракушки,
paheeskAHt' rAHkooshkee,

look for little seashells,

построить замок из песка,
pahstrOYeet' zAHmahk ees pihskAH,

build a sand castle,

понаблюдать за птицами?
pahnahblyoodAHt' zah ptEEtsahmee?

watch (observe) the birds?

Ты хочешь лечь (на подстилку) ?
Tui khAWchihsh lyehch'
(nah pahdstEElkoo)?

Do you want to lie down (on the blanket)?

116

Смотри за/ сестрой/ братом/.
SmahtrEE zah/ sihstrOY/ brAHtahm/.

Watch your/ sister/ brother/.

Я останусь здесь и буду /за ним/
за ней/ смотреть.
Yah ahstAHnoos' zdyehs' ee bOOdoo
zah neem/ zah nyehy/ smahtrYEHt'/.

I'll stay here and watch/
him/ her/.

Ты хочешь загореть?
Tui khAWchish zahgahrYEHt?

Do you want to get a tan?

Ты сгорел/-а (на солнце). (m/f)
Tui/ sgahrYEHl/ah (nah sAWntsih).

You got sunburnt.

Где крем?
Gdyeh kryehm?

Where is the lotion?

Где очки от солнце?
Gdyeh ahchkEE awt sAWntsih?

Where are the sunglasses?

Какой прекрасный день для/
купания/ катания на лыжах/!
KahkOY prihkrAHsnuiy dyehn' dlyah/
koopAHneeyih/ kahtAHneeyih nah
lUIzhahkh/!

What a beautiful day for/
swimming/ skiing/!

Нам не нужно брать в аренду:
Nahm nih nOOzhnah braht'
vahrYEHndoo:

We don't need to rent:

лыжи,
lUIzhee,

skis,

лыжные палки,
lUIzhnuiyih pAHlkee,

ski poles,

лыжные ботинки.
lUIzhnuiyih bahtEEnkee.

ski boots.

У нас есть своё снаряжение.
Oo nahs yehst' svahYAW snahryihzh-
YEHneeyih.

We have our own equipment.

117

Моё снаряжение нужно подогнать.
MahYAW snahryihzhYEHneeyih
nOOzhnah pahdahgnAHt'.

My equipment needs to
be adjusted.

Снег слишком/ мягий/ твёрдый/.
Snyehk slEEshkahm/ mYAHkeey/
tvYAWrduiy/.

The snow is too/ soft/ hard/.

Сколько стоит билет на канатный
подъёмник?
SkAWl'kah stAWeet beelYEHt nah
kahnAHtnuiy pahdYAWmneek?

How much is a chairlift
ticket?

Где билетная касса?
Gdyeh beelYEHtnahyih kAHsah?

Where is the ticket office?

Не иди на самый верх горы!
Nih eedEE nah sAHmuiy vyerkh gahrUI!

Don't go to the top of the
mountain!

Горка слишком крутая!
GAWrkah slEEshkahm krootAHyih!

The hill is too steep!

Это опасно! Не так быстро!
EHtah ahpAHsnah! Nih tahk bUIstrah!

That's dangerous!

Туда опасно идти.
ToodAH ahpAHsnah eetEE.

It's dangerous to go
there.

Какой форм!
KahkOY fawrm!

What form!

Тебе холодно?
TihbYEH khAWlahdnah?

Are you cold?

Мне/ холодно/ жарко/ тепло/.
MnYEH/ khAWlahdnah/ zhAHrkah/
tihpklAW/.

I am/ cold/ hot/ warm/.

Ты устал/-а? (m/f)
Tui oostAHl/-ah?

Are you tired?

Хорошо бы сейчас выпить чего-
-нибудь/ горячего/ тёплого/.
KhahrahSHAW bui sihchAHs vUIpeet'
chihvAW-neeboot'/ gahrYAHchihvah/
tyAWplahvah/.

It would be nice to have
something/ hot/ warm/ to
drink.

Давайте (pl) зайдём вовнутрь –
DahvAHytyih zahydYAWm vahvnOOtr' –

Let's go inside –

    чтобы отдохнуть,
    shtAWbui ahtdahkhnOOt',

       to rest,

    чтобы поесть,
    shtAWbui pahYEHst',

       to eat,

    чтобы согреться.
    shtAWbui sahgrYEHt'sah.

       to warm up.

Когда мы/ уходим/ уезжаем/?
KahgdAH mui/ ookhAWdeem/ ooyehzh-
AHihm/?

When are we leaving?

Пора идти домой.
PahrAH eetEE dahmOY.

It is time to go home.

Упаковывай свои вещи.
OopahkAWvuivahy svahEE vYEHschee.

Pack up your things.

Я уже/ готов/ готова/: (m/f)
Yah oozhYEH/ gahtAWf/ gahtAWvah/.

I'm ready:

    идти,
    eetEE,

       to go,

    идти гулять,
    eetEE goolYAHt',

       to go for a walk,

    есть.
    yehst'.

       to eat.

Ну, уж если идти, так сейчас.
Noo, oozh YEHslee eetEE, tahk
sihchAHs.

Well, if we're going, let's
go now.

Будет сильное движение.
BOOdiht sEEl'nahyih dveezhYEHn-
eeyih.

There will be a lot of traffic.

Смотри, чтобы у тебя всё (с собой)
было.
SmahtrEE, shtAWbui oo tihbYAH
fsyaw (sahbOY) bUIlah.

Make sure that you have
everything (with you).

Тебе было весело?
TihbYEH bUIlah vYEHsihlah?

Did you have a good time?

Мне было весело.
MnYEH bUIlah vYEHsihlah.

I had a good time.

Мне весело.
MnYEH vYEHsihlah.

I'm having a good time.

Out of Sight, Out of Mind!

С глаз долой, из сердца вон!

Восклицания	Exclamations
Ой! Awy!	Ouch! Oops! Ow!
Ну что же?! Noo shtawzh?!	What?!
Оп-пля! Ahp-lyah!	Up/ down/ you go!
Нет проблем! Nyeht prahblYEHm!	No problem!
Хорошо! Всё в порядке! KhahrahshAW! Fsyaw fpahrYAHdkyih!	All right! Okay!
Давай! DahvAHy!	Go ahead! (permission)

121

Здорово! Прекрасно!
ZdAWrahvah! PrihkrAHsnah!

Great!

Вот это дело!
Vawt EHtah dYEHah!

Now you're talking!

Как глупо!
Kahk glOOpah!

How silly!

Тебе /радостно/ весело/?
TihbYEH/ rAHdahsnah/ vYEHsihlah/?

Are you/ sad/ happy/?

Мы рады, что ты победил/-а. (m/f)
Mui rAHdui, shtaw tui pahbihdEEl/-ah.

We're glad that you won.

Помоги(те)! (s/pl)
PahmahgEE (tyih)!

Help!

Не рискуй!
Nih reeskOOy!

Don't take risks!

Я буду/ осторожен/ остарожна/. (m/f)
Yah bOOdoo/ ahstahrAWzhihn/ ahstah-
rAWzhnah/.

I'll be careful.

Кто виноват?
Ktaw veenahvAHt?

Whose fault is it?

Мне жаль. Это моя вина.
MnYEH zhahl'. EHtah mahYAH
veenAH.

I'm sorry. It's my fault.

Тут ничего не сделаешь.
Toot neechihVAW nih zdYEHlahihsh.

It can't be helped.

Я ничего не могу поделать!
Yah neechihVAW nih mahgOO
pahdYEHlaht'!

I can't help it!

Ничего не помогает!
NeechihvAW nih pahmahgAHiht!

Nothing's helping!

Я сдаюсь!
Yah zdahYOOs'!

I give up!

Вот как!
Vawt kahk!

Is that so!

Это не так!
EHtah nih tahk!

That's not so!

Безусловно это так!
ByihzooslAWvnah EHtah tahk!

It certainly is!

Как хочешь!
Kahk khAWchihsh!

As you wish!

Прежде всего...
PrYEHzhdyih fsyihvAW...

First of all...

Почему так долго?
PahchihmOO tahk dAWlgah?

Why is it taking so long?

Нет, вы видали такое!
Nyeht, vui veedAHlee tahkAWeh!

Well, what do you know!
(Expressing surprise!)

Какая очередь!
KahkAHyah AWchihriht!

What a line!

Вот как?
Vawt kahk?

Really?

Я верю тебе.
Yah vYEHryoo tihbYEH.

I believe you.

Можешь надеяться на меня.
MAWzhihsh nahdYEHyiht'sah nah
mnYAH.

You can count on me.

Ничего страшного.
NeechihvAW strAHshnahvah.

It's no big deal.

Делай, как хочешь.
DYEHlahy, kahk khAWchish.

Do as you like.

Мне всё равно!
MnYEH fsyaw rahvnAW!

I don't care!

Отдыхай! (or) Отдохни!
AhtduikhAHy! (or) Ahddahkhnee!

Relax!

Будь/ разумен/ разумна/. (m/f)
Boot'/ rahzOOmihn/ rahzOOmnah/.

Be reasonable.

Почему ты отказываешься/ играть/
говорить/?
PahchihmOO tui ahtkAHzuivahihshsah/
eegrAHt'/ gahvahrEEt'/?

Why do you refuse to/
play/ speak/?

Пусть будет по-твоему.
Poost' bOOdiht pah-tvAWihmoo.

Have it your way.

Ты меня не понимаешь.
Tui mnYAH nih pahneeMAHihsh.

You don't understand me.

Мне всё равно.
MnYEH fsyaw rahvnAW.

It's all the same to me.

Давай покончим с этим.
DahvAHy pahkAWncheem sEHteem.

Let's get this over with.

Это не твоё дело.
EHtah nih tvahYAW dYEHlah.

That doesn't concern you.

С каких пор?
SkahkEEkh pawr?

Since when?

Я это тебе сто раз говорил/-а. (m/f)
Yah EHtah tihbYEH staw rahz gahvah-
rEEl/-ah.

I've told you a hundred
times.

Откуда мне знать?
AhtkOOdah mnYEH znaht'?

How should I know?

124

Кто знает?
Ktaw znAHiht?

Who knows?

Это (не) важно.
EHtah (nih)vAHzhnah.

That's (not) important.

Конечно! Конечно нет!
KahnYEHshnah! KahnYEHshnah nyeht!

Of course! Of course not!

Это уж слишком.
EHtah oosh slEEshkahm.

That's going too far.

Ни в коем случае! (or) Ни за что!
Nee fkAWihm slOOchahih! (or) Nyee
zah shtaw!

No way!

Это правда или ты всё это
придумал/-а. (m/f)
EHtah prAVdah EElee tui fsyaw EHtah
preedOOmahl/-ah?

Is that true or did you
make up that story?

Правильно!
PrAHveel'nah!

Correct!

Безусловно!
ByihzooslAWvnah!

Sure!

Всё равно дела не поправишь.
Fsyaw rahvnAW dYEHlah nih
pahprAHveesh.

There's nothing you
can do about it.

Тем лучше.
Tyem lOOchih.

So much the better.

Всё к лучшему.
Fsyaw klOOtshihmoo.

It's all for the best.

Я точно не знаю.
Yah tAWchnah nih znAHyoo.

I'm not certain.

Я/ согласен/ согласна/ (с тобой). (m/f)
Yah/sahglAHsihn/ sahglAHsnah/ (stahbOY).

I agree (with you).

Я тоже.
Yah tAWzhyih.

So do I.

Это очень интересно.
EHtah AWchihn' ihntihrYEHsnah.

It's very interesting.

Ты очень смешной мальчик!
Tui AWchihn' smihshnOY mAHl'cheek!

You're a very funny boy!

Ты очень смешная девочка!
Tui AWchihn' smyihshnAHyih dYEH-vahchkah!

You're a very funny girl!

Как смешно! Это не смешно!
Kahk smyihshnAW! EHtah nih smyihshnAW!

How funny! That is not funny!

Вздор!
Vzdawr!

Nonsense!

Везёт! Не везёт!
VihzYAWt! Nih vihzYAWt!

In luck! Out of luck!

Тебе везёт!(pres) Тебе повезло!(past)
TihbYEH vihzYAWt! TihbYEH pahvihzlAW!

Lucky you!

Как ужасно!
Kahk oozhAHsnah!

How awful!

Очень жаль.
AWchihn' zhahl'.

That's too bad.

Как жаль!
Kahk zhahl'!

What a pity!

Это невероятно!
EHtah nihvihrahYAHtnah!

That is unbelievable!

Замечательно!
ZahmihchAHtihl'nah!

Wonderful! Marvelous!

Очень хорошо. Отлично.
AWchihn' khahrahshAW. AhtlEEchnah.

Very good. Excellent.

Это ты так только пошутил/-а? (m/f)
EHtah tui tahk tAWl'kah pahshoo-
tEEl/-ah?

You were just joking,
weren't you?

Не шути.
Nih shootEE.

Don't joke.

Я спрашиваю серьёзно.
Yah sprAHsheevahyoo sihr'YAWznah.

I'm asking seriously.

Надеюсь, что/ да/ нет/!
NahdYEHyoos', shtaw/ dah/ nyeht/!

I hope/ so/ not/!

Я думаю, что/ да/ нет/!
Yah dOOmahyoo, shtaw/ dah/ nyeht/!

I think /so/ not/!

Как бы не так!
Kahk bui nih tahk!

I should say not!

А-а, понятно!
AH-ah, pahnYAHtnah!

Oh, I see!

Это ясно?
EHtah YAHsnah?

Is that clear?

Не беспокойся! (or) Не волнуйся!
Nih byihspahkOYsah! Nih vahlnOOysah!

Don't worry!

Всякое /бывает/ случается!
FsYAHahyih/ buivAHiht/ sloochAHihtsah/!

Accidents happen!

Не бойся (собаку).
Nih bOYsah (sahbAHkoo).

Don't be afraid (of
the dog).

Успокойся!
OospahkOYsah!

Calm down!

Ради Бога!   For heaven's sake!
RAHdee bAWgah!

Не сердись.   Don't be angry.
Nih sihrdEEs'.

Ну, ничего, ничего...   There, there...
Noo, neechihvAW, neechihvAW...

Всё будет нормально.   Everything will be all
Fsyaw bOOdiht nahrmAHl'nah.   right.

Если я могу это сделать, то и ты   If I can do it, then you
сможешь.   can do it.
YEHslee yah mahgOO EHtah
zdYEHlaht', taw ee tui smAWzhihsh.

Это (не) правильно.   It's (not) right/ just/ fair/.
EHtah (nih) prAHveel'nah.

Это не обязательно.   That's not necessary.
EHtah nih ahbyihzAHtihl'nah.

Не вздумай!   You'd better not!
Nih vzdOOmahy!

Убери руки!   Hands off!
OobyihrEE rOOkee!

Ну и беспорядок!   What a mess!
Noo ee byihspahrYAHdahk!

Довольно! (or) Хватит!   Enough of that!
DahvAWl'nah! (or) KhvAHteet!

Мне надоело!   I'm fed up!
MnYEH nahdahYEHlah!

Что мне делать?   What am I to do?
Shtaw mnYEH dYEHlaht'?

Не мешай мне.
Nih mihshAHy mnYEH.

Don't disturb me.

У меня не было ни одной свободной
минуты!
Oo mnYAH nYEH builah nee ahdnOY
svahbAWdnoy meenOOtui!

I haven't had a moment
to myself!

Что надо сделать?
Shtaw nAHdah zdYEHlaht'?

What's to be done?

В чём дело?
Fchyawm dYEHlah?

What's the matter?

Это правда, не так ли?
EHtah prAHvdah, nih tahk lee?

That's true, don't you
think?

Ты знаешь, ...
Tui znAHihsh, ...

You know, ...

Ну конечно!
Noo kahnYEHshnah!

Yes, indeed!

Не может быть! Неужели?
Nih mAWzhiht buit! NihoozhYEHlee?

You don't say! Really?

Как обычно.
Kahk ahbUIchnah.

As usual.

Будь здоров/-а (m/f)!
Boot' zdahrAWf/ zdahrAWvah/!

Bless you!

Что такое?
Shtaw tahkAWeh?

What's wrong?

Ничего.
NeechihvAW.

Never mind.

Я был/-а неправ/-а. (m.f)
Yah buil/ builAH nihprAHf/ nihprAHvah/.

I was wrong.

EXCLAMATIONS

Почему ты жалуешься?
PahchihmOO tui zhAHlooishsah?

Why are you complaining?

Осторожно!
AhstahrAWzhnah!

Look out! Watch out!

Сейчас же!
SihchAHs zheh!

Right now!

Опасно! Осторожно!
AhpAHsnah! AhstahrAWzhnah!

Danger! Caution!

Господи! Боже мой!
GAHspahdee! BAWzhih moy!

Goodness gracious!

Это дело нешуточное!
EHtah dYEHlah nihshOOtahshnahyih!

This is no laughing matter!

Над чем ты смеёшься?
Naht chyem tui smihYAWshsah?

What are you laughing at?

Не смейся.
Nih smYEHysah.

Don't laugh.

Так тебе и надо!
Tahk tihbYEH ee nAHdah!

It serves you right!

Тебе нельзя так говорить!
TihbYEH nihl'zYAH tahk gahvahrEEt'!

You must not say that!

Господи! О Боже!
GAHspahdee! Ah, BAWzhih!

My God! Oh, God!

Это очень большой!
EHtah awchihn' bahl'shOY!

It's immense!

Хорошо. Можно.
KhahrahshAW. MAWzhnah.

That's fine.

Дело в шляпе!
DYEHlah fshlYAHpih!

It's in the bag! (hat)

Я тоже! (or) И я!
Yah tAWzhih! (or) Ee yah!

Me too!

Что ты хочешь этим сказать?
Shtaw tui khAWchihsh EHteem
skahzAHt'?

What do you mean by this?

Что ты пытаешься сказать?
Shtaw tui puitAHihshsah skahzAHt'?

What are you trying to say?

Скажи то, что думаешь.
SkahzhEE taw, shtaw dOOmahihsh.

Say what you think.

Это всё! (or) Больше нет!
EHtah fsyaw! BAWl'shih nyeht!

That's all! All gone!

Вот и всё!
Vawt ee fsyaw!

It's over! That's all!

... во что бы то ни стало!
... vah shtaw bui taw nee stAHlah!

...no matter what happens!

Not the gift is dear, love is dear.

Не дорог подарок, дорога любовь
Празднование дня рождения Birthday Party

С днём рождения!
Zdnyawm rahzhdYEHneeyih!

Happy Birthday!

Какой подарок ты хочешь на день
рождения?
KahkOY pahdAHrahk tui khAW-
chihsh nah dyehn' rahzhdYEHneeyih?

What kind of present would
you like for your birthday?

Это для тебя. (or) Это тебе.
EHtah dlyah tihbYAH. (or) EHtah tihbYEH.

This is for you.

Тебе бы хотелось устроить вечеринку
на день своего рождения?
TihbYEH bui khahtYEHlahs oostrOY-
eet' vihchihrEEnkoo nah dyehn' svahyihvAW rahzhdYEHneeyih?

Would you like to have a
birthday party?

Мы будем отмечать твой день
рождения в субботу.
Mui bOOdihm ahtmıhchAHt' tvoy
dyehn' rahzhdYEHneeyih fsoobAWtoo.

We'll celebrate your
birthday on Saturday.

Мы пригласим твоих друзей.
Mui preeglahsEEm tvahEEkh droozYEHy.

We'll invite your friends.

Мы можем пригласить всех моих друзей?
Mui mAWzhihm preeglahsEEt' fsyekh mahEEkh droozYEHy?

Can we invite all my friends?

Может быть мы устроим пикник!
MAWzhiht buit' mui oostrOYeem peeknEEk!

Maybe we could have a picnic!

У нас будут: (pl.)
Oo nahs bOOdoot:

We'll have:

трубочки с мороженым,
trOObahchkee smahrAWzhihnuim,

ice cream cones,

воздушные шары, шляпы,
vahzdOOshnuiyih shahrUI, shlYAHpui,

balloons, hats,

игры, подарки.
EEgrui, pahdAHrkee.

games, presents.

У нас будет торт. (sing.)
Oo nahs bOOdiht tawrt.

We'll have cake.

Где ты хочешь устроить вечеринку?
Gdyeh tui khAWchihsh oostrOYeet' vihchihrEEnkoo?

Where do you want to have the party?

дома, в парке,
dAWmah, fpAHrkyih,

at home, in the park,

в ресторане, на пляже?
frehstahrAHnyih, nah plYAHzhih?

in a restaurant or at the beach?

Я купил/-а тебе открытку и подарок.
Yah koopEEl/-ah tihbYEH ahtkrUItkoo ee pahdAHrahk. (m/f)

I bought you a card and a present.

Сколько тебе лет? Я не знаю.
SkAWl'kah tihbYEH lyeht? Yah nih znAHyoo.

How old are you? I don't know.

Мне/ пять/ десять/ лет.
MnYEH/ pyaht'/ dYEHsyiht'/ lyeht.

I am/ five/ ten/ years old.

Когда твой день рождения?
KahgdAH tvoy dyehn' rahzhdYEHneeyih?

When is your birthday?

Мой день рождения десятого мая.
Moy dyehn' rahzhdYEHneeyih dyehs-YAHtahvah mAHyih.

My birthday is on May 10.

Чего бы тебе хотелось больше всего?
ChihvAW bui tihbYEH khahtYEHlahs' bAHl'shih fsyihvAW?

What do you wish the most?

Кем ты будешь (когда вырастешь)?
Kyehm tui bOOdihsh (kahgdAH vUI-rahstihsh)?

What will you be? (when you grow up)

Кем ты хочешь стать, когда вырастешь?
Kyehm tui khAWchihsh staht', kahg-dAH vUIrahstihsh?

What do you want to be when you grow up?

Я буду учителем, пожарным.
Yah bOOdoo oochEEtihlyihm, pahzhAHrnuim.

I will be a teacher, fireman.

Я буду/ богатым (m)/ богатой (f)/.
Yah bOOdoo/ bahgAHtuim/ bahgAHtoy/.

I will be rich.

Сколько свечек?
SkAWl'kah svYEHchihk?

How many candles?

Давайте(pl) их сосчитаем!
DahvAHytyih eekh sahscheetAHihm!

Let's count them!

Задуй свечки!
ZahdOOy svYEHchkee!

Blow out the candles!

Порежь торт!
PahrYEHzh' tawrt!

Cut the cake!

Подели торт на шесть кусков.
PahdyehlEE tawrt nah shyehst' kooskAWf.

Divide the cake into six pieces.

Я хотел/-а бы: (m/f)
Yah khahtYEHl/-ah bui:

I'd like:

шоколадного мороженого,
shahkahlAHdnahvah mahrAWzhihnahvah,

(some) chocolate ice cream,

персикового мороженого,
pYEHrseekahvahvah mahrAWzhihnahvah,

(some) peach ice cream,

ванильного мороженого.
vahnEEl'nahvah mahrAWzhihnahvah.

(some) vanilla ice cream..

Что ты получил/-а в подарок?
Shtaw tui pahloochEEl/-ah fpah-
dAHrahk?

What did you receive for a present?

Все дарят имениннику много подарков.
Fsyeh dAHryiht eemihnEEnneekoo
mnAWgah pahdAHrkahf.

Everyone gives a lot of presents to the birthday person.

Спасибо за подарок.
SpahsEEbah zah pahdAHrahk

Thanks for the gift.

Какая замечательная вечеринка!
KahkAHyah zahmihchAHtihl'nahyah
vihchihrEEnkah!

What a great party!

Теперь мне можно получить
водительские права?
TihpYEHr' mnYEH mAWzhnah
pahloochEEt' vahdEEtihl'skeeyih
prahvAH?

Now can I get my driver's license?

sleep is better than medicine.

Сон лучше всякого лекарства

Пора спать   Bedtime

This is a good time to read a story in Russian to your child. The language he hears before going to sleep will linger in his mind during the night. This might also be a golden opportunity to learn and recite prayers in Russian.

Какой зевок!   What a yawn!
KahkOY zihvAWk!

Ты зеваешь.   You're yawning.
Tui zihvAHihsh.

Ты/ устал/-а? (m/f)   Are you tired?
Tui/ oostAHl/-ah/?

Ты хочешь спать?   Are you drowsy ?
Tui khAWchihsh spaht'?

(Тебе) пора спать.   Time (for you) to go to bed.
(TihbYEH) pahrAH spaht'.

Ты /должен (m) /должна (f) /идти спать.   You should go to bed.
Tih/ dAWlzhihn/ dahlzhnAH/ eetEE spaht`.

136

Ещё рано!
YihschYAW rAHnah!

It's still early!

Не ложись сегодня поздно спать.
Nih lahzhEEs' sihvAWdnyih pAWznah
spaht'.

Don't stay up late tonight.

Я уложу тебя спать.
Yah oolahzhOO tihbYAH spaht'.

I'm putting you to bed.

Мне уже надо идти спать?
MnYEH oozhYEH nAHdah eetEE
spaht'?

Do I have to go to bed
already?

Иди и принеси (свою) книгу.
EedEE ee preenihsEE (svahYOO)
knEEgoo.

Go get your book.

Расскажи мне рассказ.
RahskahzhEE mnYEH rahskAHs.

Tell me a story.

Я прочитаю тебе рассказ,
Yah prahcheetAHyoo tihbYEH rahskAHs,

I'll read you a story,

...перед тем как ты пойдёшь спать.
...PYEHRiht tyehm kahk tui pahy-
dYAWsh spaht'.

...before you go to bed.

Однажды...(or) Давным-давно...
AhdnAHzhdui...(or) DahvnUIm-
dahvnAW...

Once upon a time....

Ты смотришь телевизор?
Tui smAWtreesh tihlihvEEzahr?

Are you watching TV?

Сними/ одежду/ обувь/.
SneemEE/ ahdYEHzhdoo/ AWboof'/.

Take off your/ clothes/
shoes/.

Надень пижаму.
NahdYEHn' peezhAHmoo.

Put on your pajamas.

137

Повесь свою рубашку.
PahvYEHs' svahYOO roobAHshkoo.

Hang up your shirt.

Подбери свою одежду!
PahtbihrEE svahYOO ahdYEHzhdoo!

Pick up your clothes!

Эти носки нужно выстирать.
EHtee nahskEE nOOzhnah
vUIsteeraht'.

These socks need to be washed.

Ты готов/-а идти спать? (m/f)
Tui /gahtAWf/ gahTAWvah/ eetEE
spaht'?

Are you ready for bed?

Приготовься.
PreegahtAWv'sah.

Get ready.

Я уже/ готов/ готова/. (m/f)
Yah oozhYEH/ gahtAWf/
gahtAWvah/.

I'm ready.

Пожелай папе „Спокойной ночи."
PahzhihlAHy pAHpih „SpahkOYnoy
nAWchee."

Say, "Good Night" to Daddy.

Ты/ произнёс/ произнесла/ молитву?
Tui/ praheeznYAWs/ praheeznihslAH/
mahlEEtvoo? (m/f)

Did you say your prayers?

Ты становишься тяжёлым/ой! (m/f)
Tui stahnAWveeshsah tyihzhYAWl-
uim/ tyihzhYAWloy!

You're getting heavy!

Закрой глаза.
ZahkrOY glahzAH.

Close your eyes.

Ложись. Ляг.
LahzhEEsh. Lyahk.

Lie down.

Тише, пожалуйста.
TEEshih, pahzhAHloostah.

Quiet, please.

Тебе нужно/ лежать в постели/ спать/.
TihbYEH nOOzhnah / lihzhAHt'
fpahstYEHlee/ spaht'/.

You must/stay in bed/
sleep/.

Я тебя накрою.
Yah tihbYAH nahkrAWyoo.

I'll cover you up.

Ты ещё не в кровати?
Tui yihschYAW nih fkrahvAHtee?

You're not in bed yet?

Сейчас не слишком рано идти спать!
SihchAHs nih slEEshkahm rAHnah
eetEE spaht'!

It's not too early to go
to bed now!

Ты хочешь, чтобы свет был включён?
Tui khAWchihsh, shtAWbui svyeht
buil vklyoochAWn?

Do you want the light lit?

Мама тебя любит!
MAHmah tihbYAH lYOObeet!

Mommy loves you!

Ты мокрый/ мокрая? (m/f)
Tui mAWkruiy/ mAWkrahyih?

Are you wet?

У тебя режутся зубы.
Oo tihbYAH rYEHzhootsah zOObui.

You're teething.

Ты/ проснулся/ проснулась? (m/f)
Tui/ prahsnOOlsah/ prahsnOOlahs'?

Did you wake up?

Ты не спишь?
Tui nih speesh?

Are you awake?

Ты спишь?
Tui speesh?

Are you asleep?

Почему ты не ещё спишь?
PahchihmOO tui nih yihschYAW speesh?

Why aren't you asleep yet?

Я хочу ещё поспать.
Yah khahchOO yihschYAW
pahspAHt'.

I want to sleep a little
longer.

BEDTIME

Тебе не спится? TihbYEH nih spEEtsah?	Can't you sleep?
Не разбуди/ его/ её/! Nih rahzboodEE/ yihvAW/ yihYAW/!	Don't awaken/ him/ her/!
Чего ты хочешь,/ мой малыш/ моя малышка/? ChihvAW tui khAWchish,/ moy mahl'-UIsh/ mahYAH mahl'UIshkah/? (m/f)	What do you want, my little one?
У тебя царапина на колене. Oo tihbYAH tsahrAHpeenah nah kahlYEHnyih.	You have a scratch on your knee.
Ты нездоров/-а? (m/f) Tih /nihzdahrAWf/ neezdahrAWvah/?	Aren't you well?
У тебя болит/ живот/ животик/? Oo tihbYAH bahlEEt/ zheevAWt/ zheevAWteek/?	Do you have a/ stomach/ tummy/ ache?
От чего тебе стало нехорошо? Awt chihvAW tihbYEH stAHlah nihkhahrahshAW?	What made you sick?
У тебя кружится голова? Oo tihbYAH krOOzheetsah gahlahvAH?	Do you feel dizzy?
Голова кружится. GahlahvAH krOOzheetsah.	I'm dizzy.
У тебя температура? Oo tihbYAH tihmpihrahtOOrah?	Do you have a fever?
У тебя болит/ голова/ зуб/? Oo tihbYAH bahlEEt/ gahlahvAH/ zoop/?	Do you have a/ headache/ toothache/?
У меня (сильно) болит голова. Oo mnYAH (sEEl'nah) bahlEEt gahlahvAH.	I have a (bad) headache.

Не тряси головой.
Nih tryihsEE gahlahvOY.

Don't shake your head.

У меня болят зубы.
Oo mnYAH bahlYAHt zOObui.

My teeth hurt.

У тебя (есть) сыпь.
Oo tihbYAH (yehst') suip'.

You have a rash.

У тебя опухли железы.
Oo tihbYAH ahpOOkhlee zhYEHlihzui.

Your glands are swollen.

Высуни язык!
VUIsoonee yihzUIk!

Stick out your tongue!

Покажи язык.
PahkahzhEE yihzUIk.

Show your tongue

У тебя начинается грипп.
Oo tihbYAH nahcheenAHihtsah greep.

You're getting the flu.

Я/ Ты/ простудился/ простудилась/.
Yah/ Tui/ prahstoodEElsah/ prahstoo-
dEElahs'/. (m/f)

I/ You/ have caught a cold.

Ты/ кашляешь/ чихаешь/.
Tui / kAHshlyahihsh/ cheekhAHihsh/.

You're/ coughing/
sneezing/.

У тебя болит горло?
Oo tihbYAH bahlEEt gAWrlah?

Do you have a sore
throat?

Я измерю тебе температуру.
Yah eezmYEHryoo tihbYEH tihmp-
ehrahtOOroo.

I'll take (measure) your
temperature.

У тебя/ жар/ кашель/.
Oo tihbYAH/ zhahr/ kAHshihl'/.

You have a/ fever/ cough/.

Тебе нужно что-то от кашля.
TihbYEH nOOzhnah shtaw-tah awt
kAHshlyih.

You need something for
the cough.

141

Тебе нужно принимать лекарство
(от кашля).
TihbYEH nOOzhnah preeneemAHt'
lihkAHrstvah (awt kAHshlyih).

You have to take your
(cough) medicine .

Завтра тебе нужно оставаться в постели.
ZAHvtrah tihbYEH nOOzhnah ahstah-
vAHt'sah fpahstYEHlee.

Tomorrow you'll have to
stay in bed.

Тебе необходимо как следует отдохнуть.
TihbYEH nihahbkhahdEEmah kahk
slYEHdooiht ahtdahkhnOOt'.

You have to get a good rest.

У тебя что-нибудь болит?
Oo tihbYAH shtAW-neeboot' bahlEEt?

Does something hurt?

У тебя болит/ рука/ нога/?
Oo tihbYAH bahlEEt/ rookAH/
nahgAH/?

Does your/ arm/ foot/ hurt?

Ты уколол/-а палец? (m/f)
Tui ookahlAWl/-ah pAHlihts?

Did you prick your finger?

Ты хочешь пластырь?
Tui khAWchihsh plAHstuir'?

Do you want a bandaid?

Ты хорошо спал/-а? (m/f)
Tui khahrahshAW spahl/-AH?

Did you sleep well?

(Почему) ты плохо себя чувствуешь?
(PahchihmOO) tui plAWkhah sihbYAH
chOOstvooihsh?

(Why) do you feel bad?

Ты хорошо себя чувствуешь?
Tui khahrahshAW sihbYAH chOOstvooihsh?

Do you feel good?

Когда я буду лучше себя чувствовать?
KahgdAH yah bOOdoo lOOchih
sihbYAH chOOstvahvaht'?

When will I feel better?

Тебе скоро будет лучше.
TihbYEH skAWrah bOOdiht
lOOchih.

You'll feel better soon.

Выздоравливай!
VuizdahrAHvleevahy!

Get better!

Можно мне переночевать у (...........) ?
MAWzhnah mnYEH pihrihnahchih-
vAHt' oo (name Gen.)?

May I sleep at (name)'s
house?

Можно (name) у нас переночевать?
MAWzhnah (name Dat.) oo nahs pihrih-
nahchihvAHt'?

May (name) sleep over at
our house?

Произнеси молитву.
PraheeznihsEE mahlEEtvoo.

Say your prayers.

Тебе удобно?
TihbYEH oodAWbnah?

Are you comfortable?

Спи спокойно!
Spee spahkOYnah!

Sleep well!

Тссс!
Tsss!

Shhh!

Приятных сновидений!
PreeYAHtnuikh snahveedYEHneey!

Sweet dreams!

Morning gray -- a pretty day.

Серенькое утро, красненький денёк

Погода   The Weather

Try sharing a picture book about weather with your child and discuss the pictures using Russian. This could be more of a "school" kind of chapter if you and your child want to play school. Flash cards to make, maps to draw, temperatures to record, fun to be had!

Как красиво!   How beautiful!
Kahk krahsEEvah!

Какой чудесный день!   What a lovely day!
KahkOY choodYEHsnuiy dyehn'!

Облаков нет.   There are no clouds.
AhblahkAWf nyeht.

Солнечно.   It is sunny.
SAWnnyehchnah.

144

Солнце светит.
SAWntsih svYEHteet.

The sun's shining.

Сегодня пасмурно.
SihvAWdnyih pAHsmoornah.

It's overcast today.

Сегодня (очень) жарко.
SihvAWdnyih (AWchihn') zhAHrkah.

It's (very) hot today.

Тепло. Лето.
TihplAW. LYEHtah.

It's warm. It's summer.

У нас период сильной жары.
Oo nahs pihreeAWt sEEl'noy zhahrUI.

We're having a heat wave.

Нет ни малейшего ветерка.
Nyeht nee mahlYEHyshihvah vihtihrkAH.

There's not a bit of wind.

Я потею.
Yah pahtYEHyoo.

I'm sweating.

/Ветрено./ Облачно/.
/VYEHtrihnah/ AWblahchnah/.

It's/ windy/ cloudy/.

(Слегка) прохладно. Холодновато.
(SlihkAH) prahkhlAHdnah.
KhahlahdnahvAHtah.

It's (a bit) cool. It's a bit cold.

Становится сыро.
StahnAWveetsah sUIrah.

It's getting damp.

Тебе нужна куртка./ Тебе нужен свитер.
TihbYEH nzhnAH kOOrtkah./
TihbYEH nOOzhihn svEEtihr.

You need a/ jacket/ sweater/.

(Опять) идёт дождь.
(AhpYAHt') ihdYAWt dawzht'.

It's raining (again).

Посмотри на/ дождь/ снег/.
PahsmahtrEE nah/ dawzht/ snyehk/.

Look at the/ rain/ snow/.

На улице лужи.
Nah OOleetsih lOOzhee.

There are puddles in the street.

У тебя мокрые туфли.
Oo tihbYAH mAWkruiih tOOflee.

Your shoes are wet.

Какая сегодня ужасная погода!
KahkAHyah sihvAWdnyih oozhAHs-
nahyah pahgAWdah!

What awful weather today!

Это ливень.
EHtah lEEvihn'.

It's a shower.

Сегодня высокая влажность.
SihvAWdnyih vuisAWkahyah
vlAHzhnahst'.

The humidity is high today.

Скоро будет светло.
SkAWrah bOOdiht svyehtlAW.

It will be light soon.

Небо/ тёмное/ серое/.
NYEHbah/ tYAWmnahyih/ sYEHrahyih/.

The sky is/ dark/ gray/.

Скоро будет темно.
SkAWrah bOOdiht tihmnAW.

It will soon be dark.

/Гремит гром. /Сверкает молния/.
/GrihmEEt grawm. /SvihrkAHiht
MAWlneeyih/.

It's/ thundering/ lightening/.

Идёт град.
EedYAWt graht.

It's hailing.

Какая гроза!
KahkAHyah grahzAH!

What a storm!

Какой туман!
KahkOY toomAHn!

What fog!

Стоит туман.
StahEEt toomAHn.

It's foggy.

Подожди, пока не пройдёт дождь.
PahdahzhdEE, pahkAH nih prahy-
dYAWt dawzht'.

Wait until the rain stops.

Ты видишь радугу?
Tui vEEdeesh rAHdoogoo?

Do you see the rainbow?

Начинает идти снег!
NahcheenAHiht eetEE snyehk!

It's beginning to snow!

Идёт снег.
EedYAWt snyehk.

It's snowing.

Похоже, идёт/ дождь/ снег/.
PahkhAWzhih, eedYAWt/ dawzht/
snyehk/.

It looks like it's/ raining/
snowing/.

Снежинки падают!
SnyezhEEnkee pAHdahyoot!

Snowflakes are falling!

Погода (совсем) как зимой!
PahgAWdah (sahfsYEHm) kahk zeemOY!

It's (really) wintry weather!

Как сверкает снег!
Kahk svihrkAHiht snyehk!

How the snow sparkles!

Может быть, мы сможем слепить
снеговика.
MAWzhiht buit', mui smAWzhihm
slihpEEt' snyihgahveekAH.

Perhaps we can build a
snowman.

/Дождь/ снег/ перестал.
/Dawzht'/ snyehk/ pihrihstAHl.

The/ rain/ snow/ has stopped.

Снег тает.
Snyehk tAHiht.

The snow is melting.

better late than never.

Лучше поздно, чем никогда

Время	Time
Который час? KahtAWree chahs?	What time is it?
Сколько времени...? SkAWl'kah vrYEHmihnee...?	How much time...?
Сейчас час. SihchAHs chahs.	It is one o'clock.
Сейчас/ два/ три/ четыре/ часа. SihchAHs/ dvah/ tree/ chihtUIree/ chahsAH.	It is / two/ three/ four/ o'clock .
Сейчас/ пять/ шесть/ семь/ часов SihchAHs/ pyaht'/ shehst'/ syehm'/ chahsAWf.	It is/ five/ six/ seven/ o'clock.
Сейчас четверть четвёртого. SihchAHs chYEHtvyehrt' chyehrt- vYAWrtahvah.	It is quarter after three.

148

Сейчас двадцать минут седьмого.
SihchAHs dvAHdtsaht' meenOOt
syihd'mAWvah.

It is six twenty.

Сейчас без четверти семь.
SihchAHs byehs chYEHtvihrtee syehm'.

It is quarter of seven.

Сейчас без двадцати семь.
SihchAHs byehs dvahtsahtEE syehm'.

It is twenty of seven.

Сейчас восемь часов.
SihchAHs vAWsihm' chahsAWf.

It is eight o'clock.

Сейчас девять часов.
SihchAHs dYEHviht' chahsAWf.

It is nine o'clock.

Сейчас половина десятого.
SihchAHs pahlahvEEnah dyihsYAHt-
ahvah.

It is nine thirty.

Сейчас десять минут одиннадцатого.
SihchAHs dYEHsiht' meenOOt
ahdEEnnahtsahtahvah.

It is ten after ten (o'clock).

Сейчас одиннадцать часов.
SihchAHs ahdEEnahtsaht' chahsAWf.

It is eleven o'clock.

Сейчас половина первого.
SihchAHs pahlahvEEnah pYEHrvahvah.

It is twelve thirty.

Сейчас/ ночь/ полночь/.
SihchAHs/ nawch/ pAHlnawch/.

It is/ night/ midnight/.

Сейчас/ день/ полдень/.
SihchAHs/ dyehn'/ pAHldyehn'/.

It is/ day/ noon/.

Сейчас/ утро/ вторая половина дня/
вечер/.
SihchAHs/ OOtrah/ ftahrAHyah pahlahvEEnah dnyah/ vYEHchihr/.

It's/ morning/ afternoon/
evening/.

149

Рано/ Поздно/.
/RAHnah/ pAWznah/.

It is/ early/ late/.

Длится/ давно/ недавно/.
DlEEtsah/ dAHvnah/ nihdAHvnah/.

It lasts a/ long/ short/ time.

Как можно/ скорей/ скорее/.
Kahk mAWzhnah/ skahrYEHy/ skahrEYih/.

As soon as possible.

Как только ты захочешь.
Kahk tAWlkah tui zahkhAWchihsh.

As soon as you want.

В будущем....
FbOOdooschihm...

In the future...

Two heads are better than one.

Один ум хорошо, а два лучше

<table>
<tr><td>

Количество

Сколько лет/ сестре/ маме/ папе/?
SkAWl'kah lyeht/ sihstrYEH/
mAHmih/ pAHpih/?

Сколько пальцев ты видишь?
SkAWl'kah pAHl'tsihf tui vEEdeesh?

Сколько?
SkAWl'kah ?

Есть (только)/ один/ четыре/.
Yehst' (tAWl'kah)/ ahdEEn/ chihtUIree/.

У меня нет ничего.
Oo mnYAH nyeht neechihvAW.

Ничего нет!
NeechihvAW nyeht!

Всё печенье съели!
Fsyaw pihchYEHn'ih sYEHlee!

</td><td>

Quantities

How old is/ sister/ mommy/
daddy/?

How many fingers do you
see?

How many are there?

There is (only)/ one/ four/.

I have none.

There is nothing!

All the cookies have been
eaten!

</td></tr>
</table>

151

После семи идёт восемь.
PAWslih sihmEE eedYAWt vAWsihm'.

After seven comes eight.

Считай от трёх до десяти.
ScheetAHy awt tryawkh dah dihsyihtEE.

Count from 3 to 10.

Продолжай считать.
PrahdahlzhAHy scheetAHt'.

Continue counting.

Один плюс один – два.
AhdEEn plyoos ahdEEn – dvah.

One and one makes two.

Сколько будет пять минус два?
SkAWl'kah bOOdiht pyaht' mEEnoos
dvah?

How much is five minus
two?

Четыре минус один – три.
ChihtUIree mEEnoos ahdEEn – tree.

Four minus one is three.

Дважды два – четыре.
DvAHzhdui dvah – chihtUIree.

Two times two equals four.

Сорок разделить на пять – восемь.
SAWrahk rahzdihlEEt' nah pyaht' –
vAWsihm'.

Forty divided by five
makes eight.

Два, четыре, и шесть – чёртные числа.
Dvah, chihtUIree, ee shyehst' –
chYAWrt nuiih chEEslah.

Two, four and six are even
numbers.

Три, пять, и семь – нечёртные числа.
Tree, pyaht', ee syehm' –
nihchYAWrtnuiih chEEslah.

Three, five and seven
are uneven numbers.

Две половины.
Dvyeh pahlahvEEnui.

Two halves.

Дроби: половина, треть, четверть, три четверти.
DrAWbee: pahlahvEEnah, tryeht', chYEHtvihrt', tree chYEHtvihrtee.

Fractions: a half, a third, a fourth, three-fourths.

немного/ меньше/ больше/
nihmnAWgah/ mYEHn'shih/ bAWl'shih/

a little/ less/ more/

несколько
NYEHskahl'kah

some, a few, several

много
mnAWgah

many, a lot

ноль	0	четырнадцать	14
один	1	пятнадцать	15
два	2	шестнадцать	16
три	3	семнадцать	17
четыре	4	восемнадцать	18
пять	5	девятнадцать	19
шесть	6	двадцать	20
семь	7	двадцать один	21
восемь	8	двадцать два	22
девять	9	двадцать три	23
десять	10	тридцать	30
одиннадцать	11	тридцать один	31
двеннадцать	12	тридцать два	32
тринадцать	13	тридцать три	33

сорок	40		девяносто	90
сорок один	41		девяносто один	91
сорок два	42		девяносто два	92
сорок три	43		девяносто три	93
пятьдесят	50		сто	100
пятьдесят один	51		сто один	101
пятьдесят два	52		сто два	102
пятьдесят три	53		сто три	103
шестьдесят	60		двести	200
шестьдесят один	61		двести один	201
шестьдесят два	62		двести два	202
шестьдесят три	63		двести три	203
семьдесят	70		триста	300
семьдесят один	71		триста один	301
семьдесят два	72		триста два	302
семьдесят три	73		триста три	303
восемьдесят	80		четыреста	400
восемьдесят один	81		четыреста один	401
восемьдесят два	82		четыреста два	402
восемьдесят три	83		четыреста три	403

пятьсот	500	девятьсот	900
пятьсот один	501	девятьсот один	901
пятьсот два	502	девятьсот два	902
пятьсот три	503	девятьсот три	903
шестьсот	600	тысяча	1000
шестьсот один	601	две тысячи	2000
шестьсот два	602	три тысячи пятьсот	3500
шестьсот три	603		
семьсот	700	десять тысяч	10,000
семьсот один	701	сто тысяч	100,000
семьсот два	702	миллион	1,000,000
семьсот три	703	два миллиона	2,000,000
восемьсот	800	миллиард	1,000,000,000
восемьсот один	801		
восемьсот два	802		
восемьсот три	803		

Note: **Boldface** letters in the numbers above indicate the stressed syllable.

Repetition is the mother of learning.

Повторенье — Мать ученья

Алфавит					Alphabet	
А	Б	В	Г	Д	Е	Ё
ah	beh	veh	geh	deh	ye	yo
Ж	З	И	Й	К	Л	М
zheh	zeh	ee	ee(short)	kah	el	em
Н	О	П	Р	С	Т	У
en	oh	peh	err	ess	teh	oo
Ф	Х	Ц	Ч	Ш	Щ	Ъ
ef	kha	tseh	cheh	shah	shchah	(hard sign)
Ы	Ь	Э	Ю	Я		
B"i"ll	(soft sign)	eh	yoo	yah		

Какая это буква ?
KahkAHyih EHtah bOOkvah?

What letter is this?

Вот буква А.
Vawt bOOkvah ah.

Here is the letter A.

156

Назови эту букву.
NahzahvEE EHtoo bOOkvoo.

Name this letter.

Сколько букв в слове "кошка"?
SkAWl'kah bookf fslAWvyih
"kAWshkah"?

How many letters are in the word "cat"?

Где буква "Н"?
Gdyeh bOOkvah "en"?

Where is the letter "N"?

Скажи слово "легко" по буквам.
SkahzhEE slAWvvah "lihkAW"
pah bOOkvahm.

Spell the word "easy."

Покажи букву "Г."
PahkahzhEE bOOkvoo "geh."

Point to the letter "G."

Что значит это слово?
Shtaw znAHchiht EHtah slAWvah?

What does this word mean?

Тебе нужно вычеркнуть это слово.
TihbYEH nOOzhnah vUIchihrknoot'
EHtah slAWvah.

You have to cross out this word.

Чьё это имя?
Chyaw EHtah EEmyih?

Whose name is this?

Не держи так крепко карандаш.
Nih dihrzhEE tahk krYEHpkah kahrahndAHsh.

Don't hold the pencil tightly.

Держи его вот так. Пиши вот так.
DihrzhEE yihvAW vawt tahk. PeeshEE
vawt tahk.

Hold it like this. Write like this.

Ты умеешь писать?
Tui oomYEHihsh peesAHt'?

Do you know how to write?

Я умею писать.
Yah oomYEHyoo peesAHt'.

I know how to write.

157

what you sow you shall reap.

Что посеешь, то и пожнёшь

Детские песенки　　　　　Nursery Rhymes

Nursery rhymes are a marvelous way to soothe a crying baby, or just enjoy for their own rhythm.. Trusting that the reader already knows the English version of these rhymes, we have chosen to translate them more closely to the Russian text so that, even though stilted at times, the literal translation of the Russian words will be understood by the reader.

У Маши был барашек

Mary Had a Little Lamb

У Маши был барашек,
Барашек, барашек,

Mary had a little lamb
a little lamb, a little lamb,

У Маши был барашек
С шёрсткой, словно снег.

Mary had a little lamb,
with wool like snow.

Куда бы Маша ни пошла,
Ни пошла, ни пошла,

Wherever Mary went,
Mary went, Mary went,

Куда бы Маша ни пошла
Барашек ходит с ней.

Wherever Mary went,
the lamb goes with her.

Дождик, дождик, уходи

Дождик, дождик, уходи
Послезавтра приходи.
Разве трудно перестать?
Ваня хочет поиграть.

Rain, Rain Go Away

Rain, rain, go away.
After tomorrow come back.
Is it really difficult to stop?
Johnny wants to play.

Пётр и Егорка

Пётр и Егорка
Полезли на горку,
Тащили ведёрко с водою.
Егорка свалился
И лбом приложился.
Петра потащил за собою.

Peter and Yegor (Jack and Jill)

Peter and Yegor
Climbed up a hill
Dragging a bucket with water.
Yegor fell down
With his head hitting the ground
Dragging Peter along (with him).

Прошу я звёздочку

Прошу я звёздочку мерцать,
Я так хочу её понять.
Над высоким миром, там,
Как алмаз сияет нам.
Прошу я звёздочку мерцать,
Я так хочу её понять.

I Ask a Little Star
(Twinkle Twinkle Little Star)

I ask a little star to twinkle,
I so want to understand it.
High above the earth, there,
Like a diamond it glows to us.
I ask a little star to twinkle,
I so want to understand it.

Просыпайся

Просыпайся, просыпайся,
Брат Антон, брат Антон.
Утро в колокольчик,
Утро в колокольчик
– Динь, динь, дон.
– Динь, динь, дон.

Wake up   (Brother John)

Wake up, wake up,
Brother John, Brother John.
The morning at the bell,
The morning at the bell,
Ding, Ding, Dong.
Ding, Ding, Dong.

Шалтай - Болтай

Humpty Dumpty

Шалтай - Болтай сидел на стене,
Шалтай - Болтай свалился во сне.
Ни царские кони,
ни царская рать
Не могут Шалтая - Болтая собрать.

Humpty Dumpty sat on a wall,
Humpty Dumpty fell down in sleep.
Neither the king's cavalry,
nor the king's array
Were able to assemble Humpty
Dumpty.

Школьник, школьник,

Ten O'clock Scholar (School boy)

Школьник, школьник,
Что так рано
Ты спешишь
Сегодня в класс?
Ты всегда
Приходишь в восемь,
А теперь
Десятый час!

Scholar, scholar,
What so early.
You are hurrying
Today to class?
You always
Arrive at eight,
But now
Nine o'clock has struck!

Джек был героем

Jack Was a Hero
(Jack Be Nimble)

Джек был героем —
Он через свечку
Прыгнул однажды,
Забравшись на печку.

Jack was a hero —
He over a candle
Jumped once,
From the top of the stove.

В город

To Town
(To Market, To Market)

В город , в город за свиньёй
Я иду пешком.
Возвращаюсь я домой
На свинье верхом!

To town, to town for a pig
I am going by foot.
I return homeward
Astride of the pig!

160

Шалунишки– котятки

Шалунишки– котятки
        потеряли перчатки
И не смеют взойти на порог.
— Мама, мама, прости!
Мы не можем найти,
Куда подевались перчатки!
— Не найдёте перчатки,
так и знайте, котятки,
Я не стану готовить пирог!
Мяу-мяу пирог, мяу-мяу пирог,
Я не стану готовить пирог!

Испугались котятки,
отыскали перчатки
И к маме бегут со всех ног.

— Мама, мама, открой
и пусти нас домой!
Мы нашли на дороге перчатки!
— Отыскали перчатки?
Золотые котятки!
Получайте за это пирог!
Мяу-мяу пирог, мяу-мяу пирог,
Получайте за это пирог!

Натянули котятки
на лапки перчатки
И съели до крошки пирог.
— Ай, мамочка, ай!
Ты нас не ругай,
Но грязными стали перчатки!
— Грязнульки-котятки!
Снимайте перчатки!
Я вас посажу под замок!
Мяу-мяу под замок,
мяу-мяу под замок,
я вас посажу под замок!

Three Little Kittens

Three little kittens lost gloves

And do not dare cross the doorway.
Mama, Mama, excuse!
We cannot find,
Where we put the gloves!
If you do not find the gloves,
Be sure, kittens,
I will not fix a pie!
Meow, Meow a pie, Meow a pie,
I will not fix a pie!

The kittens were scared,
they retrieved the gloves
and ran to their Mama
as fast as they could.

— Mama, Mama open up
and let us to home!
We found our gloves on the road!
— You found the mittens?
Precious kittens!
Have your pie!
Meow, Meow a pie, Meow a pie,
Have your pie!

The kittens
put on their paws gloves
And ate until the pie is all gone.
– Ah, Mama,
don't scold us,
But our gloves have gotten dirty!
– Dirty kittens!
Take off your mittens!
I will put you under lock and key!
Meow, meow under lock and key,
Meow-meow under lock and key,
I will put you under lock and key!

Стирают котятки
в корыте перчатки.
Ах, как это трудно – стирать!
Все три, три и три –
Ой, мама, смотри!
Уже отстирались перчатки!
— Отмыли перчатки?
За это, котятки,
Я вас отпущу погулять!
Мяу-мяу погулять,
Мяу-мяу погулять,
Опять отпущу погулять!

The kittens are washing
the mittens in the tub
Oh, how difficult – to wash!
Rub, rub and rub –
Mama, look!
Already the gloves are washed!
— Cleaned gloves?
For that, kittens,
I will let you take a walk!
Meow, meow, a walk,
meow, meow a walk,
Again I will let you take a walk!

Три беленькие мышки

Три беленькие мышки
Бегут, не чуя ног,
За мельничихой старой
Вприпрыжку за порог.

Она хвосты отрезала
Им кухонным ножом
А что случилось дальше,
Я расскажу потом.

Three Blind Mice
(Three White Mice)
Three white mice
They run at top speed
From the old miller's wife
Skipping along outside
the threshold.

She cut off their tails
With a kitchen knife
And what happened further,
I'll tell later.

Баю - баю, детки

Баю - баю, детки
На еловой ветке.
Тронет ветер вашу ель —
Закачает колыбель,
А подует во весь дух —
Колыбель на землю — бух!

Rock-a-Bye Baby
(Rock-a-bye Babies)
Lullaby, of a baby.
On a spruce branch.
The wind will touch your spruce –
The cradle will rock
When blows at full speed –
The cradle to the ground – bang!

МОЛИТВЫ

Отче Наш

Отче наш, сущий на небесах,
Да святится имя Твое;
Да придет Царствие Твое;
Да будет воля твоя и на земле,
как на небе;
Хлеб наш насущный
дай нам на сей день;
и прости нам долги наши,
как и мы прощаем
должникам нашим;
и не введи нас в искушение,
но избавь нас от лукавого. Аминь.

Псалом Давида

1. Господь– Пастырь мой
я ни в чем не буду нуждаться:
2. Он покоит меня на злачных
пажитях и водит меня
к водам тихим,
3. Подкрепляет душу мою,
направляет меня на стези правды
ради имени Своего.
4. Если я пойду и долиною
смертной тени, не убоюсь зла,
потому что Ты со мною;
Твой жезл и Твой посох– они
успокоивают меня.
5. Ты приготовил
предо мною трапезу
в виду врагов моих,
умастил елеем голову мою;
чаша моя преисполнена.
6. Так, благость и милость да
сопровождают меня во все дни
жизни мой, и я пребуду в доме
Господнем многие дни.

Молитва перед едой

Благослови, Господи, все, что
по милости твоей вкушаем.
Аминь.

PRAYERS

Our Father

Our Father, who are in heaven,
hallowed be thy name; Thy
kingdom come, Thy will be
done on earth
as it is in heaven.
Our daily bread,
Give us this day;
and forgive us our trespasses
as we forgive
those who offend us
And lead us not into temptation,
but deliver us from evil. Amen.

Psalm 23

1.Lord – my shepherd,
I shall need nothing.
2. He reposes me in peace
and leads me
to quiet water.
3. He refreshes my soul.
He leads me in right paths
for the sake of His name.
4. If I go in the valley of deathly
shadow, I fear no evil;
because you are with me.
Your rod and Your staff
they soothe me.
5. You prepared
a table before me
in the sight of my foes;
You anointed my head with oil;
my cup is filled.
6. So, goodness and kindness
will accompany me all the days
of my life, and I will be in the
Lord's house many days.

Prayer before Meals

Thank you Lord for all the
kindness and nourishment
you provide. Amen.

VOCABULARY

Семья и другие лица

The Family and Other Persons

мать/ мама	mother/ mom	внук	grandson
отец/ папа	father/ dad	дочь	daughter
бабушка	grandmother	сын	son
дедушка	grandfather	сестра	sister
неродной брат	cousin (m)	брат	brother
неродная сестра	cousin (f)	женщина	woman
жена	wife	мужчина	man
муж	husband	девочка	girl
тётя	aunt	мальчик	boy
дядя	uncle	ребёнок	child
племянница	niece	господин	Mister
племянник	nephew	госпожа	Missus
внучка	grand-daughter	госпожа	Miss

Ласковые слова

Endearments

мой/ моя детка	my baby	дорогая (моя)	sweetheart
моя кукла	my doll	дружок	buddy
моя принцесса	my princess	моя малышка	my little one
мой принц	my prince	мой малыш	my little one
моё сокровище	my treasure	милый (ая)	honey, sweetie
дорогой (мой)	sweetheart	мой цыплёнок	my little chick

Цвета

Colors

зелёный	green	жёлтый	yellow
синий	blue	Фиолетовый	purple
чёрный	black	розовый	pink
белый	white	коричневый	brown
оранжевый	orange	серый	gray
красный	red	бежевый	beige

Дни недели

Days of the Week

понедельник	Monday	пятница	Friday
вторник	Tuesday	суббота	Saturday
среда	Wednesday	воскресенье	Sunday
четверг	Thursday		

Месяца

январь	January	июль	July
февраль	February	август	August
март	March	сентябрь	September
апрель	April	октябрь	October
май	May	ноябрь	November
июнь	June	декабрь	December

Времена года

весна	spring	осень	autumn
лето	summer (m)	зима	winter

Праздники года

день рождения	birthday	день Матери	Mother's Day
Новый год	New Year's	день Отца	Father's Day
деньСв. Валентина	Valentine's Day	4-е июля	July 4
Еврейская пасха	Passover	празник всех святых	Halloween
пасха	Easter	день благодарения	Thanksgiving Day
		рождество	Christmas
		сочельник	Christmas Eve

Детская комната

ванна	bath tub	ночник	night light
книга	book	пустышка	pacifier
коляска	carriage	картина	picture
детская кроватка	crib	манеж	play pen
пелёнка	diaper	горшок	potty
бутылочка	bottle	качалка	rocker
стульчик для кормления	high chair	английская булавка	safety pin
Мать Гусыня	Mother Goose	коляска	stroller
		игрушка	toy

Months of the Year

Seasons of the Year

Holidays of the Year

Nursery

166

Игрушки

мяч	ball	кисточка	paint brush
воздушный шар/	balloon	клейстер	paste
шарик		книга с картинками	picture book
бита	bat	копилка	piggy bank
бусина	bead	самолёт	plane
велосипед	bicycle	марионетка	puppet
кубик	block	пузл	puzzle
(парусная) лодка	boat (sail)	гоночный автомобиль	race car
бульдозер	bull dozer	грабли	rake
автобус	bus	погремушка	rattle
автомобиль	car	кольцо	ring
шахматная доска	chess board	ракета	rocket
глина	clay	конь-качалка	rocking
клоун	clown		horse
ковбой	cowboy	верёвка	rope
цветной	crayon	песочница	sandbox
карандаш		ножницы	scissors
кукла	doll	самокат	scooter
кукольный дом	doll house	качели	seesaw
барабан	drum	лопатка	shovel
серьга	earring	конёк	skate (ice)
удочка	fishing rod	роликовый конёк	skate(roller)
форт	fort	роликовая доска	skateboard
игра	game	санки	sled
глобус	globe	детская горка	slide
вертолёт	helicopter	солдатик	soldier
обруч	hoop	подводная лодка	submarine
труба	horn	качели	swing
индеец	Indian	танк	tank
чёртик в	jack-in-the		(military)
табакерке	box	чайный сервис	tea service
скакалка	jump rope	мишка	teddy
воздушный змей	kite	теннисная ракетка	tennis
стеклянный	marble		racquet
шарик		палатка	tent
маска	mask		
ожерелье	necklace		
набор красок	paint box		

Toys

167

юла, волчок	top	нефтевоз	oil truck
ящик для игрушек	toy box	аварийная	tow truck
трактор	tractor	машина	
поезд	train	вагон	wagon
трёхколёсный	tricycle	тачка	wheelbarrow
велосипед		свисток	whistle
грузовик	truck	ксилофон	xylophone
самосвал	dump truck		
пожарная машина	fire truck		
мусороуборочная	garbage truck		
машина			

Одежда

Clothes

рюкзак	backpack	резиновый	rubber
купальный халат	bathrobe	сапог	(boot)
купальный костюм	bathing suit	сандалия	sandal
плавки	bathing trunks	шарф	scarf
ремень	belt	рубашка	shirt
нагрудник	bib	туфля	shoe
блузка	blouse	шнурок	shoelace
сапог	boot	шорты	shorts
кепка	cap	юбка	skirt
пальто	coat	комбинация	slip
платье	dress	тапочка	slipper
перчатка	glove	кроссовки	sneakers
носовой платок	handkerchief	лыжный костюм	snow suit
шапка	hat	носок	sock
куртка	jacket	чулок	stocking
джинсы	jeans	спортивный	sweat suit
варежка	mitten	костюм	
ночная рубашка	nightgown	пуловер	sweater
пальто	overcoat	майка	tee-shirt
пижама	pajamas	галстук	tie
трусики	panties	колготки	tights
колготки	pantyhose	зонт	umbrella
штаны,брюки	pants	подштанники	underpants
сумочка, кошелёк	pocketbook		(boys)
плащ	rain coat	майка	undershirt
		нижнее бельё	underwear
		бумажник	wallet
		штормовка	windbreaker

Развлечения

луна-парк	amusement park
аквариум	aquarium
пляж	beach
бадминтон	badminton
бейсбол	baseball
баскетбол	basketball
кегельбан	bowling
поход	camping
цирк	circus
концерт	concert
езда на велосипеде	cycling
луна-парк	fairground
рыбалка	fishing
американский футбол	football
матч	game, match
гольф	golf
гимнастика	gymnastics
ходить в поход	hiking
фильм	movie
кино	movie theatre
музей	museum
парк	park

Entertainments

вечеринка	party
пикник	picnic
площадка	playground
чтение	reading
переменка	recess (school)
ресторан	restaurant
гребля	rowing
парусный спорт	sailing
ходить по магазинам	shopping
кататься на коньках	skating
футбол	soccer
спорт	sports
филателия	stamp collecting
плавание	swimming
теннис	tennis
театр	theatre
волейбол	volleyball
ходьба	walking
виндсерфинг	windsurfing
зоопарк	zoo

Тело человека

лодыжка	ankle
рука	arm
спина	back
живот	belly
пупок	belly button
щека	cheek
грудь	chest
подбородок	chin
ухо	ear
локоть	elbow
глаз	eye
бровь	eyebrow
веко	eyelid

Human Body

лицо	face
палец	finger
ноготь	finger nail
лоб	forehead
волосы	hair
рука	hand
голова	head
пятка	heel
бедро	hip
челюсть	jaw
колено	knee
нога	leg
губа	lip

рот	mouth	большой палец	thumb
шея	neck	палец на ноге	toe
нос	nose	язык	tongue
плечо	shoulder	зуб	tooth
живот	stomach	талия	waist
горло	throat	запястье	wrist

Напитки

Beverages

пиво	beer	апельсиновый напиток	orangeade
какао	cocoa		
кофе (с молоком)	coffee (with milk)	газированная вода	soda
лимонад	lemonade	чай с лимоном	tea with lemon
молоко	milk	вода	water
апельсиновый сок	orange juice	вино	wine

Ёмкости

Containers

пакет	bag	конверт	envelope
бутылка	bottle	банка	jar
ящик	box	крышка	top, cover
консервная банка	can	тюбик	tube
картонная коробка	carton	обёртка	wrapper
деревянный ящик	crate		

Десерт

Dessert

яблочный пирог	apple pie	желатин	gelatin
торт	cake	мороженое	ice cream
леденец	candy	фруктовый коктейль	milk shake
конфета	candy bar		
шоколад	chocolate	блин	pancake
печенье	cookie	пирожное	pastry
круассон	croissant	пирог	pie
заварной крем	custard	пудинг	pudding
пончик, донатс	donut	рисовый пудинг	rice pudding
		бисквит	sponge cake
		пирожок	turnover
		йогурт	yoghurt

Овощи

спаржа	asparagus	лук	onion
свёкла	beet	петрушка	parsley
брюссельская	Brussel sprout	горох	pea
капуста		перец	pepper
капуста	cabbage	картофель	potato
морковь	carrot	тыква	pumpkin
цветная капуста	cauliflower	редис	radish
сельдерей	celery	шпинат	spinach
кукуруза	corn	кабачок	squash
огурец	cucumber	стручковая фасоль	stringbean
чеснок	garlic	помидор	tomato
салат	lettuce	репа	turnip
гриб	mushroom		

Vegetables

Мясные блюда

бекон	bacon	баранья отбивная	lamb chop
курица	chicken	свиная отбивная	pork chop
сосиска	frankfurter	жаркое	roast
ветчина	ham	ростбиф	roast beef
гамбургер	hamburger	колбаса	sausage
сосиска в булке	hot dog	бифштекс	steak
нога баранья	leg of lamb	индейка	turkey

Meat

Рыбные блюда

карп	carp	сардина	sardine
треска	cod	креветка	shrimp
камбала	flounder	палтус	sole
селёдка	herring	форель	trout
омар	lobster	тунец	tuna
лососина	salmon		

Seafood

Фрукты и ягоды

яблоко	apple
яблочное пюре	applesauce
абрикос	apricot
банан	banana
ягода	berry
черника	blueberry
черешня	cherry
кокосовый орех	coconut
виноградина	grape
грейпфрут	grapefruit
виноград кисть	grapes (bunch)

Fruits and Berries

лимон	lemon
апельсин	orange
персик	peach
груша	pear
ананас	pineapple
слива	plum
чернослив	prune
изюмина, изюм	raisin/s
малина	raspberry
клубника	strawberry
мандарин	tangerine
арбуз	watermelon

Другие продукты

хлеб	bread
сдобная булка	bun
масло	butter
каша	cereal (hot)
сыр	cheese
кукурузные хлопья	cornflakes
крекер	cracker
сливки	cream
крошка	crumb
яйцо	egg
глазунья	fried eggs
яйцо вкрутую	hard boiled egg
яйцо всмятку	soft boiled egg
картофель фри	French fries
подливка	gravy
мёд	honey
джем	jam, jelly
варенье	jam
кетчуп	ketchup
картофельное пюре	mashed potatoes
майонез	mayo
молочный шоколад	milk chocolate
горчица	mustard

Other Foods

макароны	noodles
овсяные хлопья	oatmeal
блин	pancake
арахис	peanut
арахисовая паста	peanut butter
перец	pepper
соленье	pickle
попкорн	pop-corn
картофельные чипсы	potato chips
тыква	pumpkin
рис	rice
булочка	roll
салат	salad
соль	salt
сандвич	sandwich
(с сыром)	(with cheese)
соус	sauce
квашеная капуста	sauerkraut
суп	soup
спагетти	spaghetti
тушёное мясо	stew
сироп	syrup
тост	toast
уксус	vinegar

Кухонные принадлежности

бут<u>ы</u>лка	bottle
м<u>и</u>ска	bowl
ч<u>а</u>шка	cup
в<u>и</u>лка	fork
стак<u>а</u>н	glass
ч<u>а</u>йник	kettle
нож	knife
кр<u>у</u>жка	mug
салф<u>е</u>тка	napkin
кувш<u>и</u>н	pitcher
тар<u>е</u>лка	plate
бл<u>ю</u>до	platter

Utensils

кастр<u>ю</u>ля	pot
кастр<u>ю</u>ля	saucepan
бл<u>ю</u>дце	saucer
неглуб<u>о</u>кая сковоро<u>да</u>	skillet
глуб<u>о</u>кая тар<u>е</u>лка	soup plate
л<u>о</u>жка	spoon
ск<u>а</u>терть	tablecloth
стол<u>о</u>вая л<u>о</u>жка	tablespoon
ч<u>а</u>йник	teapot
ч<u>а</u>йная л<u>о</u>жка	teaspoon
подн<u>о</u>с	tray

Дом

черд<u>а</u>к	attic
з<u>а</u>дняя дверь	back door
подв<u>а</u>л	basement
в<u>а</u>нная	bathroom
сп<u>а</u>льня	bedroom
потол<u>о</u>к	ceiling
труб<u>а</u>	chimney
стол<u>о</u>вая	dining room
дверь	door
сем<u>е</u>йная к<u>о</u>мната	family room
заб<u>о</u>р	fence
флаг	flag
пол	floor
вх<u>о</u>дн<u>а</u>я дверь	front door
сад	garden
кал<u>и</u>тка	gate

House

прих<u>о</u>жая	hallway
шланг	hose
к<u>у</u>хня	kitchen
газ<u>о</u>н	lawn
разбр<u>ы</u>згиватель	lawn sprinkler
гост<u>и</u>ная	living room
почт<u>о</u>вый <u>я</u>щик	mail box
кр<u>ы</u>ша	roof
к<u>о</u>мната	room
л<u>е</u>стница	stair
ступ<u>е</u>нька	step
унит<u>а</u>з	toilet
подс<u>о</u>бка	utility room
стен<u>а</u>	wall
окн<u>о</u>	window
двор	yard

Жил<u>и</u>ще

кварт<u>и</u>ра	apartment
б<u>у</u>нгало	bungalow
котт<u>е</u>дж в лес<u>у</u>	cabin
кооперат<u>и</u>вная кварт<u>и</u>ра	condominium

Dwellings

д<u>а</u>ча	country house
гост<u>и</u>ница	hotel
пал<u>а</u>тка	tent
приц<u>е</u>п	trailer, mobile home

Кухня

Kitchen

передник	apron	швабра	mop
метла	broom	духовка	oven
шкафчик для уборки	broom closet	ведро	pail
		кастрюля	pot
шкаф	cabinet,cupboard	скороварка	pressure cooker
часы	clock		
стенной шкаф	closet	холодильник	refrigerator
стиральная машина	clothes washer	швейная машина	sewing machine
компьютер	computer		
стол для готовки	counter	раковина	sink
моющее средство	detergent	губка	sponge
тряпка	dish cloth	табуретка	stool
посудомоечная машина	dish washer	плита	stove
		сито	strainer
тряпка для пыли	dust cloth	стол	table
совок для мусора	dustpan	тостер	toaster
веничек	egg beater	пылесос	vacuum cleaner
воронка	funnel		
утюг	iron	воск	wax
гладильная доска	ironing board		
микроволновка	microwave oven		

Ванная комната

Bathroom

аспирин	aspirin	духи	perfume
банное полотенце	bath towel	пудра	powder
ванна	bathtub	бритва	razor
щётка для волос	brush	электробритва	razor(electric)
одеколон	cologne	шампунь	shampoo
расческа	comb	раковина	sink
личное полотенце	face cloth	мыло	soap
крем для лица	face cream	бумажная салфетки	tissues
фен	hair dryer	унитаз	toilet
губная помада	lipstick	туалетная бумага	toilet paper
лак для ногтей	nail polish	зубная щётка	toothbrush
бумажное полотенце	paper towel	зубная паста	toothpaste

Спальня

		Bedroom	

Спальня / Bedroom

кресло	armchair	лампа	lamp
кровать	bed	абажур	lampshade
покрывало	bedspread	матрас	mattress
ночной столик	bedside table	зеркало	mirror
одеяло	blanket	подушка	pillow
жалюзи	blinds	наволочка	pillow case
ковёр	carpet	розетка	outlet(electric)
стул	chair	лоскутное одеяло	quilt
часы	clock	кресло-качалка	rocking chair
вешалка	coat hanger	простыня	sheet
занавеска	curtain	ставень	shutter
туалетный столик	dresser		

Гостиная / Living Room

кондиционер	air-conditioner	проигрыватель для компакт-дисков	CD player
кресло	arm chair	письменный стол	desk
книжная полка	book shelf	камин	fireplace
книжный шкаф	bookcase	пианино	piano
ковёр	carpet	картина	picture
диван	couch	радио	radio

Инструменты / Tools

топор	ax	пила	saw
молоток	hammer	ножницы	scissors
шланг	hose	винт	screw
лестница	ladder	отвёртка	screwdriver
газонокосилка	lawn mower	лопата	shovel
гвоздь	nail	мастерок	trowel
гайка	nut	тиски	vise
вилы	pitchfork	тачка	wheelbarrow
плоскогубцы	pliers	гаечный ключ	wrench
грабли	rake		
наждачная бумага	sandpaper		

175

Машина The Car

акселератор	accelerator	зеркало обзора	mirror
тормоз	brakes	заднее стекло	rear window
бампер	bumper	сиденье	seat
приборная панель	dashboard	стартёр	starter
дверь	door	руль	steering wheel
мотор	engine	противосолнечный	sun visor
бардачок	glove	козырёк	
	compartment	шина	tire
фара	headlight	багажник	trunk
капот	hood	колесо	wheel
гудок	horn	ветровое стекло	windshield
зажигание	ignition	дворник	windshield
домкрат	jack		wiper

Магазины Stores

булочная	bakery	рыбный рынок	fish market
банк	bank	цветочный магазин	florist
парикмахерская	barber shop	мебельный магазин	furniture store
салон красоты	beauty shop	заправочная станция	gas station
мясной магазин	butcher shop	гастроном	grocery store
химчистка	cleaners	скобяной магазин	hardware store
магазин одежды	clothing store	ювелирный магазин	jewelry store
магазин диетических	dairy store	прачечная	laundromat
продуктов		склад	lumber yard
магазин деликатесов	deli	лесоматериалов	
универмаг	department store	питомник	nursery
аптека	drugstore	обувной магазин	shoe store
		магазин игрушек	toy store

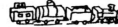

Профессии Occupations

астронавт	astronaut	мясник	butcher
(приходящая) няня	baby sitter	плотник	carpenter
пекарь	baker	шофёр	chauffeur
парикмахер	barber	уборщица	cleaning lady
водитель (автобуса)	(bus) driver		

повар	cook	медбрат (m)	nurse
молочник	dairy man	медсестра (f)	nurse
молочница	dairy woman	маляр	painter
магазина деликатесов	deli shop owner	фармацевт	pharmacist
		пилот	pilot
зубной врач	dentist	полицейский	policeman
врач	doctor	женщина-	police-
инженер	engineer	полицейский	woman
фермер	farmer	священник	priest
пожарник	fireman	гонщик	race car driver
автомеханик	garage mechanic	моряк	sailor
мусорщик	garbage man	продавец	salesman
садовник	gardener	продавщица	saleswoman
бакалейщик	grocer	секретарь	secretary
парикмахер	hairdresser	таксист	taxi driver
домашняя хозяйка	housewife	учитель	teacher
ювелир	jeweler	учительница	teacher
адвокат	lawyer	машинист	train engineer
библиотекарь(m/f)	librarian	билетёр (m)	usher
горничная	maid	билетёрша (f)	usherette
почтальон	mailman	официант	waiter
торговец	merchant	официантка	waitress
священник	minister	работник зоопарка	zoo keeper
манекенщик (m)	model		
манекенщица (f)	model		

Насекомые

Insects

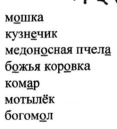

муравей	ant	мошка	gnat
шмель	bumblebee	кузнечик	grasshopper
бабочка	butterfly	медоносная пчела	honey bee
гусеница	caterpillar	божья коровка	lady bug
цикада	cicada	комар	mosquito
таракан	cockroach	мотылёк	moth
сверчок	cricket	богомол	praying mantis
стрекоза	dragonfly		
блоха	flea	паук	spider
муха	fly	оса	wasp

Дер**е**вья

Деревья	**Trees**		
яблоня	apple	грушевое дерево	pear
берёза	birch	сосна	pine
черешня	cherry	сливовое дерево	plum
фруктовое дерево	fruit tree	тополь	poplar
болиголов	hemlock	секвойа	sequoia
клён	maple	ель	spruce
дуб	oak	ива	willow

Животные	**Animals**		
медведь	bear	лама	llama
бык	bull	крот	mole
верблюд	camel	обезьяна	monkey
кошка	cat	мышь	mouse
курица	chick	вол	ox
корова	cow	свинья	pig
крокодил	crocodile	поросёнок	piglet
олень	deer	пони	pony
собака	dog	щенок	puppy
осёл	donkey	заяц	rabbit
утка	duck	енот	raccoon
слон	elephant	крыса	rat
молодой олень	fawn	северный олень	reindeer
лиса	fox	петух	rooster
пудель	French poodle	тюлень	seal
лягушка	frog	овца	sheep
жираф	giraffe	змея	snake
козёл	goat	белка	squirrel
горилла	gorilla	тигр	tiger
гусь	goose	индюк	turkey
морская свинка	guinea pig	черепаха	turtle
хомяк	hamster	кит	whale
гиппопотам	hippotamus	волк	wolf
лошадь	horse	червь	worm
ягнёнок	lamb	(земляной)	(earth)
леопард	leopard	зебра	zebra
лев	lion		

178

Птицы

дрозд	blackbird	сова	owl
синяя птица	bluebird	попугай	parrot
канарейка	canary	павлин	peacock
кардинал	cardinal	пеликан	pelican
цыплёнок	chick	пингвин	penguin
курица	chicken	фазан	pheasant
ворона	crow	голубь	pigeon
утка	duck	ворон	raven
утёнок	duckling	зарянка	robin
орёл	eagle	чайка	seagull
гусь	goose	воробей	sparrow
гусёнок	gosling	аист	stork
колибри	hummingbird	ласточка	swallow
жаворонок	lark	лебедь	swan
соловей	nightingale	индюк	turkey
страус	ostrich	дятел	woodpecker

Birds

Цветы

азалия	azalea	ландыш	lily of the valley
лютик	buttercup		
гвоздика	carnation	мимоза	mimosa
первоцвет	cowslip	хризантема	mum
шафран	crocus	орхидея	orchid
нарцисс	daffodil	анютины глазки	pansy
георгин	dahlia	пион	peony
маргаритка	daisy	петуния	petunia
одуванчик	dandelion	рододендрон	rhododendron
гардения	gardenia	роза	rose
герань	geranium	подсолнечник	sunflower
ирис	iris	душистый горошек	sweet pea
сирень	lilac	тюльпан	tulip
лилия	lily	фиалка	violet

Flowers

Вдоль доро́ги

Along the Road

аэропо́рт	airport	моторо́ллер	motorscooter
небольша́я ава́рия	breakdown	ста́вить на стоя́нку	to park
мост	bridge	пешехо́д	pedestrian
зда́ние	building	по́чта	post office
многокварти́рный дом	apartment building	доро́га	road
		доро́жный знак	road sign
зда́ние под о́фисы	office building	тротуа́р	sidewalk
авто́бус (шко́льный)	bus (school)	снегоубо́рочный комба́йн	snowplow
авто́бусная ста́нция	bus station	снего́ход	snow mobile
		ограниче́ние ско́рости	speed limit
авто́бусная остано́вка	bus stop	спорти́вная маши́на	sports car
маши́на	car	у́лица	street
це́рковь	church	у́личный фона́рь	street light
у́гол	corner	такси́	taxi
бордю́р	curb	телефо́нная бу́дка	telephone booth
скоростна́я автостра́да	expressway	телефо́нный столб	telephone pole
		пути́ (железнодоро́жные)	tracks (railroad)
фа́брика	factory	движе́ние	traffic
забо́р	fence	кольцева́я транспо́ртная развя́зка	traffic circle
по́ле	field		
пожа́рное депо́	fire house		
пожа́рный насо́с	fire plug	про́бка	traffic jam
спу́щенная ши́на	flat tire	светофо́р	traffic light
жива́я и́згородь	hedge	по́езд	train
автостра́да	highway	вокза́л	train station
е́хать автосто́пом	hitch-hiking	грузови́к	truck
дом	house	авари́йная маши́на	tow truck
почто́вый я́щик	mail box	тунне́ль	tunnel
мопе́д	moped	микроавто́бус	van
мотоци́кл	motorbike, motorcycle		

Pronunciation Guide

The pronunciation guide represents only an approximation of the Russian sounds, as it is almost impossible to give auditory equivalents from written English. Not all the sounds of all the Russian letters are given here. This guide is a very basic one intended as a quick reference.

Our best advice is to speak with a Russian accent, and enjoy yourself!

Russian Vowel	English Sound	Pronunciation	Russian Word	Kids Stuff
Stressed **a**	**a** as in father	ah	дать	daht'
Unstressed **a**	(a weaker **a**)	ah	давать	dahvAHt'
Stressed **я**	**ya** as in **yacht**	yah	пять	pyaht'
Unstressed **я**	**yi** as in **yippee**	yih	январь	yihnvAHr'
э	**e** as in **echo**	eh	это	EHtah
Stressed **e**	**ye** as in **yes**	yeh	нет	nyeht
Unstressed **e**	**i** as in **sit** (or)	ih	сестра	sihstrAH
	yi as in **yield**	yih	его	yihvAW
ы	**y** as in **merry**	ui	ты	tui

Russian Vowel	English Sound	Pronunciation	Russian Word	Kids Stuff
и	ee as in see	ee	или	EElee
Stressed o	aw as in awful	aw	перо	pihrAW
Unstressed o	a as in father	ah	когда	kahgdAH
ё	yaw as in yawn	yaw	ещё	yihschYAW
у	oo as in cool	oo	улица	OOleetsah
ю	you as in youth	yoo	юбка	YOOpkah

Note: Where stressed and unstressed are not stated, it is to be inferred that they are similar sounds.

Russian Consonant	English Sound	Phonetic Symbol	In final position:
б	b as in boat банк	b	sounds like p хлеб khlehp
в	v as in vat вот	v	sounds like f рабов rahbAWf
г	g as in goat гол	g	sounds like k друг drook
д	d as in dog дать	d	sounds like t вид veet
ж	s as in measure жена	zh	sounds like sh муж moosh
з	z as in zoo за	z	sounds like s без byes

Russian Consonant	English Sound	Phonetic Symbol	
к	**k** as in **k**ing класс	**k**	(Voiceless *)
л	**l** as in **l**oaf лампа	**l**	
м	**m** as in **m**om мой	**m**	
н	**n** as in **n**o нас	**n**	
п	**p** as in **p**apa парк	**p**	(Voiceless *)
р	**r** as in **r**un раз	**r**	
с	**s** as in **s**un сам	**s**	(Voiceless *)
т	**t** as in **t**oe так	**t**	(Voiceless *)
ф	**f** as in **f**un Футбол	**f**	(Voiceless *)
х	**ch** as in lo**ch** хлеб	**kh**	
ц	**ts** as in **ts**ar царь	**ts**	
ч	**ch** as in **ch**eer читать	**ch**	
ш	**sh** as in **sh**op шляпа	**sh**	(Voiceless*)

Russian Consonant	English Sound	Phonetic Symbol
щ	**sch** as in **sh**eep ве**щь**	**sch**
й	**y** as in bo**y** тво**й**	**y**
ъ	hard sign	not pronounced
ь	soft sign	not pronounced

An apostrophe (') represents the soft sign (ь) and indicates that the consonant is soft.

* Voiceless means that the vocal chords do not vibrate.

At the end of a word the *voiced consonants* б, в, г, д, ж, and з become voiceless, that is to say, б →п, в→ ф, г →к, д → т, ж → ш, з →с. Год *gawt* ; боб *bawp*; маг *mahk*; раз *rahs*.

The *voiced consonants* б, в, г, д, ж, and з also become voiceless when they immediately precede one of the voiceless consonants п, ф, к, т, с and ш.

обсуждать → ah**p**soozhdAHt

автобус → ah**ft**AWboos

ногти → nAW**kt**ee

обширная → ah**p**shEErnahyih

ложка → lAW**sh**kah

везти → veh**st**EE

водка → vAW**tk**ah

Voiceless consonants к, п, т, с, ф, and ш become voiced — г, б, д, з, в and ж — when they immediately precede one of the voiced consonants г, б, д, з, в and ж.

вокзал → vah**gz**AHl

сдать → **zd**aht

ваш брат → vah**zh** braht

INDEX

A

(to be) able	мочь 102,108,112,122,133
to ache	болеть 140
adjusted	подогнать 113,118
(to be) afraid	бояться 40,62,127
after	после 14,20,33,66,111
after	за 71,106
again	ещё раз 80
again	опять 96,145
air mattress	надувной матрас 115
airplane	самолёт 92
to be all right	всё 15
all right	хорошо 121
allowance	расходы 67
All aboard!	отправляться 97,108
allowed, may	разрешено 58, 90
animal	животное 72,103,178
another	ещё 30
another	другой 40, 52, 59
anyone	кто-нибудь 77
arm	рука 36, 42, 142
around	вокруг 106
to ask	спросить 51,58,
to ask a	91, 127
question	задать вопрос 73, 74
(to be) asleep	спить 139
attic	чердак 114
awake	не спить 139
to awaken	разбудить 140
awful	ужасный 126, 146

B

baby	ребёнок 40, 52
back	задний 100
backwards	задний ход 108
bacon	бекон 29
bad	плохой 53,142
bad	неудачный 86
bag	сумка 126
bait	наживка 113
to bake	печь 65,66,75
baking powder	разрыхлитель 66
balance	равновесие 95
ball	мяч 38,42,94,106
balloon	воздушный шар 105,133
banana	банан 31
bandaid	гластырь 142
to bang	барабан 39
barbecue	барбекю 48
barefoot	босой 59
to bark	лаять 103
bat	бита 94
bath	ванна 20
bathroom	туалет 19
battery	аккумулятор 99
beach	пляж 114, 133
to beat	взбивать 65
beautiful	красивый 78,117,144
because	потому что 38,50
become, get	становиться 80,138,145
bed	кровать 139

C

D

E

F

exhibit	выставка 112	first	первый 56
exit	выход 89	fish	рыба 72, 114
expensive	дорогой 86	fishing rod	удочка 114
eye	глаз 36,40,53,79, 104,138	floor	пол 48, 65
		to floss	прочистить 20
		flour	мука 65
F		flower	цветок 93
		flowerbed	клумба 68
face	лицо 20	flu	грипп 141
fairly	честно 97	to flush	спустить 20
to fall	выпадать 147	fog	туман 146
fast	быстро 31,39,94,95,98	to fold	складывать 66
to fasten	пристегнуть 61,92	to fold	сложить 22, 101
father	отец 36	to follow	идти 56
faucet	кран 21	to follow	следовать 105
(to be at) fault	виноватый 122	food	еда 31
feather	перо 103	foot	нога 42,85,105,142
to feed	кормить 32,61,102	to forget	забыть 20, 56
to feel	чувствовать 15,142	fork	вилка 31
to feel like	хотеться 27, 73	form	форм 118
fever	температура 140	for ward	вперёд 96
fever	жар 141	friend	друг/-а 61,91,133
few	несколько 153	to frighten	напугать 34
field	поле 91	frog	легушка 103
to fight	драться 46	from now on	впредь будь 49
to fill	налить 21,32	fuel	топливо 92
filled	полно 64	full	полный 32
Fill 'er up!	Заправьте! 99	fun	весело 111
to find	найти 57	funny	смешной 126
finger	палец 49,142,151	furniture	мебель 89
to finish	закончить 111,114	(In) future	в будущем 150
Fire!	Пожар! 105		
fire department	пожарное отделение 105		
fireman	пожарник 134		

G

G

H

H

K

kangaroo	кенгуру 103
to keep	поддерживать 95
to keep an eye on	следить 94
to kick	ударять 38,43,106
kind	милный 81
kind of	какой 132
to kiss	поцеловать 15
kitchen	кухня 44, 58
kite	воздушный змей 104
to knead	месить 66
knee	колено 21, 140
knife	нож 31,49
to know	знать 36,62,73,124, 125, 129, 134
to know how	уметь 157
to know a lesson	выучить 77

L

lake	озеро 99, 114
to land	идти на посадку 92
lap	колено 35
large	большой 36, 103
to last	длиться 150
last	последний 30
late	поздно 61,116,137, 150,160
to be late	опаздывать 62
later	скорого 16
later	потом 23
to laugh	смеяться 130
to launder	по/стирать 64
laundry	стирка 22
lawn	лужайка 67
leader	лидер 105

L

leaf	лист 68
to lean	ложиться 47
to leave	оставить 46
to leave	уходить 94
left (adv)	налево 95
left (adj)	левый 105
lesson	урок 60,73,76,77
to let	давать 26,31,37,87,95
Let go!	Отпусти! 35
Let's go	давай(те) 40,71,119
Let's go	Поедем! 111,114
Let's go	Пойдём! 111,114
letter (alpha)	букв 156,157
library	библиотека 61,112
license	водительские права 109, 135
to lie down	лечь 116,138
Lie down!	Ложись! 138
life boat	спасательная шлюпка 97
to lift	поднять 105
light	свет 22,49,57,139
light (adj)	светый 146
to light	зажигать 48,57
lightening	молния 146
like/ as	как 36,40,79,101
to like	любить 76,103
to like	нравиться 32,37,41, 80,85,89,103,109
to like (want)	хотеть 22,28,38,44,58, 67,100,114,124,132,135
list	список 82
to listen	слушать 35,53,113
(a) little	небольшой 75
(a) little	немного 31,41,86

M

P

P

R

R

S

S   S

S

S

S

200

T · T

W

to wrap	завернуть 67
to write	писать 48,78,157
wrong	неправа 129

XYZ

yard	двор 90,93,94,114
yawn	зевок 136
to yawn	зевать 136
yellow	жёлтый 100
yet, still	ещё 139
yesterday	вчера 71
yourself	себя 29,54,60
to zipper	застегнуть 25

Also by *Therese Slevin Pirz*

Kids Stuff Spanish
Kids Stuff French
Kids Stuff Italian
Kids Stuff German
Kids Stuff Inglés

ABC's of SAT's:
How One Student Scored 800 on the
Verbal SAT